PRAISE FOR GOD'S FEMINIST MOVEMENT

God's Feminist Movement will flat-out redefine feminism for this generation. I stand beside Amber as we lead our family, our friends, our church, and the countless people who dare to read this book. She is an anointed, prophetic voice for God and has my complete support as she tackles this controversial yet important subject.

RENE PICOTA
Pastor, Streams of Life Church
Winchester, VA

Amber D'Ann Picota has written an intriguing book about the place of women in the heart of the Father. In *God's Feminist Movement*, she shares the powerful testimony of her own struggles and how God's grace has restored her and her womanhood. This book confronts the misunderstood idea of submission, pointing out that submission is for both men and women and that domination is never God's will. Women who have struggled with these issues will find help and comfort in these pages.

JOE MCINTYRE
Author of *Who We Are in Christ, Throne Life*, and *The Eternal Defeat of Satan*
Senior Minister, Word of His Grace Church
Bothell, WA

Amber Picota's book is raw, real, and revelatory, just like Amber herself. Many books take one topic and drag the reader through 150 pages, but not this one! Here we find various topics addressed swiftly and clearly. Prepare to be challenged and to grow into more Kingdom truth.

DR. JONATHAN WELTON
Best-selling Author
President of Welton Academy

This is one of those books that is born in the fire of love, the womb of experience, and the heart of visionary insight. Its tender invitation to true femininity will unlock the hearts of a generation! Excellent!

DR. CHUCK CRISCO
A New Day Dawning Ministry

I have been hearing God speaking about a new movement arising in the Church today as God is anointing and promoting women in positions of greater authority and leadership. This is a fulfillment of the prophecy mentioned in Acts 2:18. This is happening right now. Amber Picota hit this on the head in her book, *God's Feminist Movement*. Get ready to cross over into a new era as women take their rightful place in advancing the Kingdom of God on Earth.

DOUG ADDISON
Author of *Understand Your Dreams Now* and *Personal Development God's Way*
InLight Connection, Los Angeles, CA
DougAddison.com

Amber has done an exceptional job at communicating what it is to be a strong, passionate, and powerful woman. She uses not only a wealth of personal experience but a strong biblical foundation to help guide you through what a true feminist movement should look like. I believe this book will help to break down common misconceptions in today's society concerning feminism as well as inspire many women on their personal journey.

Leah Valenzuela
Bethel Church, Redding

GOD'S Feminist MOVEMENT

GOD'S Feminist MOVEMENT

REDEFINING "A WOMAN'S PLACE"
FROM A BIBLICAL PERSPECTIVE

AMBER PICOTA

DESTINY IMAGE® PUBLISHERS, INC.

P.O. Box 310, Shippensburg, PA 17257-0310

"Promoting Inspired Lives."

This book and all other Destiny Image and Destiny Image Fiction books are available at Christian bookstores and distributors worldwide.

For more information on foreign distributors, call 717-532-3040.

Reach us on the Internet: www.destinyimage.com.

Cover design by Christian Rafetto
Interior design by Terry Clifton
ISBN 13 TP: 978-0-7684-0934-5
ISBN 13 EBook: 978-0-7684-0935-2

For Worldwide Distribution, Printed in the U.S.A.
3 4 5 6 / 20 19 18 17 16

ACKNOWLEDGMENTS

This book is for my sons and daughters, both natural and spiritual. I write this for them so that the Church is a different place when they are grown and leading. I hope that because of the stand I have taken, that the world will be a different place for my babies: Joseph, Alexis, Lily, and every other spiritual son/daughter that God has sent into my life.

I could not have written this book without the support of my husband. When people said I was a crazy weirdo rebellious woman for daring to mention the dreaded F word (feminist), my sweet man reassured me those are the furthest things from the truth. Rene Picota, you are my Barak. You are not afraid to go to battle with a strong, bold, and courageous woman like me. You've got some kind of moxie, and I've never met anyone like you. You empower me. I'm better because I have you. Thank you for risking it all with me, and tarnishing your reputation by hanging out with the likes of a Christian "feminist" like me.

I also want to thank a few people who have shaped me to be the woman I am today. Jonathan Welton, I learned more from you in three years than I learned in the eight I had been a Christian before attending Welton Academy. Because of you, I understand the Bible. It is no longer a book of mystery, but a marvelous and beautiful masterpiece, fully worthy of admiration. I could go on for pages and still my words would fall short of expressing the enormity of my gratitude. You are more than my teacher. You are my friend. Thank you. You and Karen are a gift to my life.

Doug Addison, I spent my whole Christian life eagerly ready to be mentored, discipled, and equipped as a leader in the body of Christ. I have hungrily devoured teachings and books, but longed for someone to come alongside me and pour into me. Nobody has ever done this like you have. You have blessed my life more than you'll ever know, and I have learned so much working with you, listening to you, and reading your books. I know for a fact that if it weren't for you, this book would have been delayed by years probably. Thank you for investing into me. You made this book possible.

CONTENTS

FOREWORD

God is currently moving powerfully in and through the lives of women—it was always His plan! In Genesis 1:27,28 He reveals that He created "man" (mankind) in His image and likeness: male and female He created them. He then blessed them **(male and female)** and commanded **them** to be fruitful, to multiply, and to have dominion. This was God's original intent and it still is. Through Christ we have been redeemed and restored to God's original intent and His Spirit is powerfully moving on women in this hour to bring them into their rightful place alongside of men—not more in importance and authority and not less...and certainly not to replace them.

The women God is calling forth to arise in this hour are gracious, humble, wise, gentle yet strong, diligent, pure in heart and in conduct, and filled with courage, justice, and faith. They are known and marked by their love. They are not rebellious, arrogant, selfish or rude. They are a "great company of women who proclaim the glad tidings" (see Psalm 68:11). This company of women will influence every sector of society. You will find them greatly influencing the world they live in through the home, workplace, education arenas, government positions, media, business, arts and entertainment, medical fields and in the church.

Amber Picota's book, *God's Feminist Movement* is a tool He will use in this hour to reveal His plan. Amber shares from her heart the very things God has illumined to her concerning His agenda to raise up His Women for such a time as this. She shares stories and personal testimonies that many who read this book will relate to. She addresses religious mindsets and adjusts distorted theologies concerning women. I believe this book will liberate many to serve the Lord with passion and confidence in their calling.

I think of Jairus' daughter being raised from the dead. She was lifeless and without motion. Jesus said, "Little girl, I say to you, arise" (Mark 5:41 NKJV)...and she did!

Jesus is heralding a command from the heavens at this very hour, "Women of God arise."....and we will...you will—for His glory.

> *He's Calling...*
> *Wake up child, it's your turn to shine.*
> *You were born for such a time as this.*
> The Anthem, Jake Hamilton

PATRICIA KING
Apostolic Leader of Woman On The Frontlines
Founder of Women In Ministry Network (WIMN)
www.woflglobal.com

INTRODUCTION

Today there is a movement going on within the Church worldwide. God is restoring the rightful heart of feminism within His people. Not a political agenda. Not an angry uprising of women yelling, "Down with the men!"

The heart of God's Feminist Movement is for men and women to be co-heirs who edify one another and advance the Kingdom together. Men and women are (both) powerful, free, and capable of leading with excellence in their own unique way. Men and women are not the same but are equally capable of leading, ruling, and reigning with Christ.

This book takes a Kingdom-minded, New Covenant-minded, non-legalistic, non-traditional, yet biblical and godly, look at the hot topics that women face:

- Dating vs. Courting

- Modesty, Purity, and Sexuality

- Women Leaders in the Church

- Submission in Marriage

- Beauty and Confidence

I have also shared much of my own story, my experiences with many of these topics, including how I came to Christ, and I take the time to examine Scripture with historical and contextual hermeneutics, digging into the original Greek in order to fully understand what the Bible has to say about these subjects. These issues are often muddled with legalism and tradition, but this book uses historical context to make the truth simple.

Chapter 1

GOD'S FEMINIST MOVEMENT?

God is doing something really special on earth right now. I see evidence and confirmation of this everywhere I look. I believe God is specifically restoring spiritual motherhood to the Body of Christ. I'm sure by now we've all heard someone refer to a person or persons as his or her "spiritual father" or "spiritual parents." What this person means is that that individual/couple has invested in and discipled him or her. I see with eyes wide open that God is calling His women to the frontlines alongside the brave men of God. He is calling the women to rise up to rule and reign as co-heirs alongside men within the Church. He has been doing this for some time now. In fact, I believe it would be completely accurate to say He has been doing that since the beginning of time, and I think there are obvious clues of that within Scripture (we'll get to that) for those who will have eyes to see.

I call this "God's Feminist Movement." Some people find that offensive, but maybe that's just because they don't know what the true heart of feminism really is. Also, maybe there are people who, when they think of the word *feminist*, have a very negative stereotype pop into their head. I realized after talking to many people, a lot of Christians hear the word *feminist* and think of an angry woman who doesn't like men and would like to control and dominate men. I want to state up front that type of attitude doesn't please the Father, and that's not what I'm about. I'm not talking about a feminist in the sense of a political agenda here. And I'm not shouting, "Down with the men!" either. I support, love, respect, and follow the leadership of many men, one of those men being my husband. The furthest thing from my mind here is degrading and disrespecting men. My heart behind this book is to set women free, but I also believe my heart is to empower both men AND women of God. I have respect for men, and we aren't doing God any favors by advocating for women while disrespecting men. We need women to rise up and lead, but we do NOT need the men of God to back down or cower behind us. The Church doesn't need only women leaders. He has called us to rule and reign *together*.

Full Definition of FEMINISM from *Merriam-Webster*:

1. the theory of the political, economic, and social equality of the sexes

2. organized activity on behalf of women's rights and interests[1]

Wikipedia's definition: "the advocacy of women's rights on the grounds of political, social, and economic equality to men."[2]

I have highlighted in bold the definition of feminism to which I am referring when I say that God is orchestrating a "feminist movement" within the Body of Christ. Depending on whom you ask, there are going to be different ideas and preconceived notions when people hear the word *feminism*. Words and their meanings evolve over time, and sometimes a word that meant one thing to one generation means something completely different to another generation. For example, the word *gay*—to one generation the word *gay* meant "happy" or "glad," yet if you ask any American teenager today what that word means to him or her, you will find that word now means "homosexual" to the vast majority of our American culture. It would seem that many Christians have decided that *feminist* is a bad word. I disagree that it's a bad word or something with which we shouldn't associate as Christians. The true heart of feminism has always been equality. I realize there are many people who have taken their eyes off that true heart, but that doesn't mean it isn't something worth reclaiming. Any time there is a movement for something good, there are going to be people who take it so far that the pendulum swings too far to the other direction. I also realize there are man-hating women who call themselves feminists out there—all the more reason for Christian men and women to be feminists; all the more reason to restore feminism to its rightful heart: full of respect and honor for men and for women.

Much of the Church is beginning to realize that we are a family. We are God's family. The head of the Church is Jesus, and within this family, we are meant to be led both by women and men, mothers and fathers. What's a family without a mom? Well, I know some families do have to make it work without a mom, but ask a child whose mother died when he or she was little if he or she felt the void in the family that the mom left. What's a family without a dad? Sadly, we do see many families that have no choice but to make it work with one parent—and God bless single parents, because it's a very hard job. A momma wasn't meant to have to bring up children all on her own, and a father wasn't meant to go it alone either. I do believe God equips single parents with a special grace and a supernatural strength when they are faced with the task of parenting alone. I saw my own mom do it, and it wasn't easy for her, even though after my parents divorced, my dad was still a big part of my life. There's something really special and complementary about a mother and a father leading a family together and raising children together. It's like they fit together. It's like they were created to work together. It's like they were created to lead together. That's because they were. God made them that way. God created men and women different, yet equal. The ground at the foot of the cross is level. Notice that in Scripture God calls us all "His children." We're His sons and daughters. We're His co-heirs. I have a lot of ground to cover here, but I'm not going to waste your time with a lot of flowery words.

Feminist doesn't have to be a dirty word. On the contrary, as a Christian feminist, I believe God is doing something really amazing within the Church today. We ought to be ridiculously excited about what He is doing. I want to partner with Him, and I hope you do too. I believe that brave Deborahs are rising up because they see the need is great. They see the harvest, they feel the call of God, and they are ready to take this land (America and the entire world) for the Kingdom of God. This is also a time during which God is summoning the Baraks. Barak was a man so bold, so masculine and courageous, that he was not afraid to let the honor of victory go to a woman. What an exciting story!

> *Now Deborah, a prophetess, the wife of Lappidoth, was judging Israel at that time. She used to sit under the palm tree of Deborah between Ramah and Bethel in the hill country of Ephraim; and the sons of Israel came up to her for judgment. Now she sent and summoned Barak the son of Abinoam from Kedesh-naphtali, and*

*said to him, "Behold, the LORD, the God of Israel, has commanded, 'Go and march to Mount Tabor, and take with you ten thousand men from the sons of Naphtali and from the sons of Zebulun. I will draw out to you Sisera, the commander of Jabin's army, with his chariots and his many troops to the river Kishon, and I will give him into your hand.'" Then Barak said to her, "**If you will go with me, then I will go; but if you will not go with me, I will not go." She said, "I will surely go with you; nevertheless, the honor shall not be yours on the journey that you are about to take, for the LORD will sell Sisera into the hands of a woman." Then Deborah arose and went with Barak to Kedesh*** (Judges 4:4-9 NASB).

There have been many Deborahs who have gone before us to get the Church where she is today, and I'm so utterly grateful for that. I do recognize that we have a long way to go, but thank God we aren't where we used to be. I thank God for the women and men who have gone before me who were not afraid to stand up for equality within the Church. There have been women before me that endured ridicule and persecution so that I could be a voice. How dare I not speak up?

There are people today calling for the modern-day Deborahs to arise, but it's really important that the Baraks also arise. Depending on who is doing the talking, Barak is sometimes painted as a sissy or a coward. I really do not see it that way at all. I think Barak saw a quality in Deborah that he knew he had to have by his side in battle. I think of him as brave, humble, and full of wisdom. Yes, I am calling for the modern-day Deborahs to arise, but I'm also calling for the modern-day Baraks to rise up as well. One piece of leadership advice I received once was that if someone brings you an idea, utilize and equip that person to fulfill that idea. I am a pastor at a church plant. If someone comes to me to say, "Amber, I had this really cool idea. So many kids go back to school each fall whose parents can't afford a nice new backpack and clothes each year. What if our church did a backpack giveaway and we gave out backpacks stuffed with school supplies to the families in our community?" well, that's awesome. You can hear the excitement in her voice. You can sense that she loves her community and wants to help. Who better to put together a team? This person is probably a visionary, and as a leader, I could strategically call this person out to head up this project. That seems like what Barak did. Deborah came to him, not with an idea, but a word from God. She was a prophetess and a judge over the land. In other words, she was already in a position of leadership. She came to Barak with a word from the Lord, and in my eyes, Barak was as manly of a man there could be when saying, "I'll go, but I need you to go fight with me."

God is not raising ONLY women up in this hour. God also is raising men up in this hour. He is calling forth the men who are not afraid to stand beside a woman and say, "She brings something to the table that I don't have." The truth is that he brings something to the table that she doesn't have either. That's why the Bible says we are to rule and reign together as co-heirs in Christ (see Rom. 8:17). We, as the Body of Christ, need one another.

> Now if **we are children, then we are heirs—heirs of God and co-heirs with Christ,** if indeed we share in His sufferings in order that we may also share in His glory (Romans 8:17).

> For all of you who were baptized into Christ have clothed yourselves with Christ. **There is neither Jew**

nor Greek, there is neither slave nor free man, there is neither male nor female; for you are all one in Christ Jesus. *And if you belong to Christ, then you are Abraham's descendants, heirs according to promise* (Galatians 3:27-29 NASB).

It is my intention with this book to address some of the really hot topics that I believe all Christian women face. Most of the topics I will cover in this book are normally driven by tradition, legalism, and man-made doctrines or rules. I believe that we should get back to the heart of God by "letting Him out of the box" and attempting to understand Scripture properly, using good historical contextual hermeneutics. It will bring freedom to many people when they truly know what God's Word has to say on these matters, as we begin to understand what certain Scriptures meant to the original writers and readers of that day. Keep in mind that the Scriptures can't mean something different to us than they did to the people who wrote them, inspired by Holy Spirit.

What I'm asking you to do is to push aside everything you think you believe and let the Word of God and the Spirit of God teach you the truth. I don't want you to take my word for anything. It is my goal to equip you to discern, think for yourself, listen to God, and hopefully help you understand Scripture more accurately.

Chapter 2

LAYING A FOUNDATION: UNDERSTANDING THE NEW AND BETTER COVENANT

Please don't skip this chapter. I love to read books; it's one of my favorite hobbies. And oftentimes if I come across a chapter that I think is boring or might not apply to me, or if I think that I already know the information in that chapter, I will just skip it entirely. Don't skip this chapter, because I doubt you've ever heard this information presented in this way before. I promise it won't be boring either. It will likely answer questions you may have had rolling around in your head for a long time.

This chapter is the foundation upon which I build everything else in this book. If I had to pick just one thing, I would undoubtedly say that understanding the New Covenant is absolutely crucial for every single Christian and especially necessary for understanding the points I make in the rest of this book. Even if you read this chapter alone, understood it, and walked away, I believe you would benefit greatly. I want to explain to you why we are no longer under the Mosaic Law of the Old Covenant but rather are under the New Covenant and, therefore, the "law of love." This is actually really, really good news for you and me because I can pretty much guarantee you that you have broken the Old Covenant in some way just TODAY.

> *For whoever keeps the whole law and yet stumbles at just one point is guilty of breaking all of it* (James 2:10).

Jesus came to earth to forge a new and better covenant, according to Hebrews.

> *But in fact the ministry Jesus has received is as superior to theirs as the covenant of which He is Mediator* [New Covenant] *is superior to the old one, since the new covenant is established on better promises* (Hebrews 8:6).

I was going to make the whole thing bold because the whole verse is just so rad, but I wanted to put emphasis to show you that the Father isn't tenderly stroking the Old Covenant (aka the Mosaic Covenant) with fondness. The New Covenant is superior to the old one, and it's established on better promises. Also, the words in brackets were added by me for clarity. Besides all of what I already stated, Hebrews describes the Old Covenant as "obsolete and soon to pass away" (some versions say "disappear") in Hebrews 8:13. But how is it that the Old Covenant was "soon to disappear"? The wording of that verse lets us know that during the time that letter was written, it had not disappeared yet. During the time that Hebrews was written, the New Covenant did exist, and so did the Old Covenant. Jesus came to earth to establish the New Covenant, and He also came to fulfill, then destroy and do away with, the Old Covenant system. The Mosaic Covenant, what we all refer to as the "Old Covenant," was destroyed in 70 AD when the Temple of Jerusalem was destroyed or else, according to Matthew 5:18, the entire Mosaic Law would still apply. Let's take a look at that verse. This is very important to understand in light of the verse we just read in Hebrews.

> *For truly, I say to you, until heaven and earth pass away, not an iota, not a dot, will pass from the Law until all is accomplished* (Matthew 5:18 ESV).

This is really very serious here. It is so vitally important to understand this, because unless heaven and earth have passed away, the law in its entirety is still in effect. Some take this verse and say that the Old Covenant Law stands forever. If that were the case, everyone would be in a really big mess because it would be impossible for us to completely adhere to the fullness of Jewish law. In order to even start to do that, we would need animal sacrifice and so much more. There are 613 laws in the Mosaic Covenant. Can we all just take a moment to breathe a sigh of relief that the New Covenant is much less complicated than the Old Covenant? We already established before, in James 2:10, that if you break one piece of that Mosaic Law, you've broken it all.

I have tattoos. I love my tattoos and have plans to get more. Every now and then I still will have a concerned Christian who will mention Leviticus 19:28 to me. Leviticus 19:28 says, *"You shall not make any cuts in your body for the dead nor make any tattoo marks on yourselves..."* (NASB). I want to take a second to explain why that verse doesn't bother me and also doesn't change my mind about getting more tattoos, because it's so relevant to what we're talking about here. This verse in Leviticus about tattoos is for the people of a particular covenant, the Mosaic Covenant. I am not a partaker of the Mosaic Covenant. You see, in our Bible that we read today, there are canons from different covenants—more covenants, actually, than just the two that I've mentioned so far, the Mosaic Covenant and the Jesus (New) Covenant. These canons tell stories, songs, and, in the case of the verse in Leviticus about tattoos, give rules for those covenant members to uphold. Normally, if someone brings this up to me, it's just because he or she loves me and is well-meaning. There's nothing wrong with that, and I enjoy explaining the covenants so I don't at all mind explaining that I don't have to abide by the law in Leviticus 19:28 any more than that person has to abide by the law right before it in Leviticus 19:27 that says not to trim the hair on the sides of one's head or the beard.

I want to share something with you that I wish every single Christian understood. This information would bring so much freedom to believers across the world. In order to explain how it's possible that the verse in Matthew 5:18 has indeed been fulfilled—reminder: *"For truly, I say to you, until heaven and earth pass away, not an iota, not a dot, will pass from the Law until all is accomplished"* (Matt. 5:18 ESV)—then it's really important to know more about the Jewish culture of the days in which these letters and Scripture were written. "But why?" you might be thinking. The reason why is this: these Scriptures we read out of our Bible cannot mean something to us that they didn't originally mean to the original writers and hearers of that verse (letter, song, etc.). Because of that, it's really imperative that we read Scripture with good historical contextual hermeneutics. This means we need to put ourselves in the writer's shoes, to the best of our ability, and ask ourselves, "To whom was he speaking? What would this have meant to the actual people to whom he was writing this? What did these phrases mean to them and to the writer?"

To better understand the culture of this day and time, I would like to introduce you to a renowned and accurate historian and scholar named Josephus, and also to a Jewish philosopher and astronomer named Maimonides. I can't literally introduce you to them, however, because they are both dead. Maimonides lived during the 1100s, and Josephus was born in Jerusalem and lived during the times in which these Scriptures I'm citing here for you were actually written. No, their writings are not sacred Scripture, nor are they contained in our Bible, but I consider them to be historical documents that help us view Scripture with a greater understanding. Surely we can all agree that there are plenty of books that hold value and insight other than the Bible. Do you own a history book? Sure you do! That's what I like to think of when I think of these books of study. They are a lot like history books, and they help us to have a fuller understanding of the culture of that day. These documents actually support the Bible, especially the writings of Josephus, by allowing us to view Scripture in its proper historical context. The Scriptures can't mean something different to us than they did to the original hearers and writers of the Word. This is called "reader relevance."

When we get down to the nitty-gritty of understanding the meaning of this verse in Matthew that says the law exists until heaven and earth pass away, we have to realize that it's not really about what the words "heaven and earth" mean to us. It's about what it meant to the writer of this passage and to the people who were listening on as Jesus said this. To the Jews of this time in history (because remember, reader relevance), the term "heaven and earth" meant "the place where heaven met earth." Upon hearing Jesus say this, they immediately would have known He was referring to the Temple. My Pawpaw used to say, "Aww, Amber D'Ann, I was just getting yer goat." Venture here with me a moment, because I'm hoping to point out how phrases can be context-specific and have different meanings depending on the culture in which they are used. Okay, can I just admit up front that I have no idea where this phrase of speech came from? But where I'm from, down in the great state of Texas, if someone is "getting your goat" it means that person is teasing or tricking you. If someone is making fun of you and trying to get a rise out of you, he or she is "trying to get your goat." I moved up farther north into Northern Virginia, and I found out very quickly that a lot of these sayings that I was raised hearing are really puzzling to people outside of my specific Texas culture in which I grew up. These phrases don't mean the same thing to them. If I tell someone up here, "Oh, I'm sorry, I was just trying to get your goat," they're going to look at me like I'm crazy and say, "I don't have a goat." They have no grid to understand this saying with which I grew up. What they don't realize is that there is no goat involved. This isn't really about a goat. This is about something else—the goat represented something to me that they can't understand. The same applies to this verse in Matthew that refers to "heaven and earth." This meant something to them that it doesn't mean to us.

In *Antiquities of the Jews,* book 3, chapter 7, Josephus writes something that undoubtedly gives us an idea of how the Temple (called a "tabernacle" in this passage) may have represented the heavens and the earth to people of this day and age:

> ...When Moses distinguished the tabernacle into three parts, and allowed two of them to the priests, as a place accessible and common, he denoted the **land (earth) and the seas,** these being of general access to all; but he set apart the third division for God, because **heaven** is inaccessible to men.[3]

Notice that Josephus wrote that Moses separated the tabernacle into three parts. One part is considered a common area because, like the earth and the seas, it is accessible to all, but the third part was a division for God because of heaven's inaccessibility to mankind (at the time). Josephus actually goes on to say even more in this piece of literature, and it just reiterates this notion that the Temple represented "heaven and earth" to the Jews of that time. You could read the whole thing—in fact, I would encourage that—and get an even better idea of just how much this really makes sense. Plus, if you love history and plan to study more about the destruction of Jerusalem, this will come in handy. For our purposes here I just want to show you enough to help you see that.

Now what did Maimonides have to say that can add some value to this conversation? Let's check that out:

> The Arabs likewise [as the Hebrew prophets] say of a person who has met with a serious accident, "His heavens, together with his earth, have been covered"; and when they speak of the approach of a nation's prosperity, they say, "The light of the sun and moon has increased," A new heaven and a new earth has been created," or they use similar phrases.[4]

This is an excerpt from Maimonides's *The Guide for the Perplexed*, though it was in Jonathan Welton's book *Raptureless* that I came about knowing this information. I also would like to list a few Bible verses here that will show you different times in our Scriptures where the words "heaven and earth" are used figuratively, not literally. I would like you to consider that this refers not to a literal heaven and earth that would pass away; rather, this was an expression that Jesus used to allude to the people listening that the old temple worship system would soon be done away with.

And I will break the pride of your power: and I will make your heaven as iron, and your earth as brass (Leviticus 26:19 ASV).

Therefore I will make the heavens to tremble, and the earth shall be shaken out of its place, in the wrath of Jehovah of hosts, and in the day of His fierce anger (Isaiah 13:13 ASV).

Although this one in Isaiah might sound like the literal heaven and earth, the verse is only speaking to the destruction of Babylon. If this language saying, "heaven and earth" is speaking of the destruction of Babylon, then I think it's not a stretch at all to say that Matthew 5:18 is also talking about the destruction of Jerusalem. Okay, one more verse, even though there are a slew of additional examples in Scripture where God used the words "heaven and earth" to describe something other than a literal heaven and earth. Also, I hope you're noticing the other common denominator here: these Scriptures are all instances where God spoke in judgment as well— judgment against Babylon in Isaiah, as we're about to read; judgment against Edom; and then, later, judgment against the Old Covenant system.

*Their slain will be thrown out, their dead bodies will stink; the mountains will be soaked with their blood. All the stars in the sky will be dissolved and **the heavens rolled up like a scroll; all the starry host will fall** like withered leaves from the vine, like shriveled figs from the fig tree. My sword has drunk its fill in the **heavens**; see, it descends in judgment on Edom, the people I have totally destroyed* (Isaiah 34:3-5).

Furthermore, First Corinthians 6:19 establishes that under the New Covenant, God intended for our physical bodies to be the new place where heaven invades the earth. Our bodies are now temples of the Holy Spirit. We are the place at which heaven meets earth. We are like walking heaven portals, releasing His Kingdom here on earth. Jesus had to get rid of that temple system because this system is clearly superior.

> *Or do you not know that your body is a temple of the Holy Spirit who is in you, whom you have from God, and that you are not your own? For you have been bought with a price: therefore glorify God in your body* (1 Corinthians 6:19-20 NASB).

That's why when Jesus met with the woman at the well and she tried to change the subject by bringing up the controversy of that day (should they be worshiping at this temple or that temple?), Jesus told her that there would soon come a day when none of that would matter anymore because they would worship in spirit and in truth (see John 4:19-24). Could it be that Jesus was alluding to the fact that He truly intended to do away with that type of temple worship by destroying the Old Covenant system and by literally destroying the Temple of Jerusalem? That's what I'm suggesting. It was the Old Covenant Law that bound them to worship in a certain place. God had a plan to no longer be confined to a temple but rather to make us His temples.

> *"Sir," the woman said, "You must be a prophet. So tell me, why is it that you Jews insist that Jerusalem is the only place of worship, while we Samaritans claim it is here at Mount Gerizim, where our ancestors worshiped?" Jesus replied, "Believe me, dear woman, the time*

is coming when it will no longer matter whether you worship the Father on this mountain or in Jerusalem. You Samaritans know very little about the One you worship, while we Jews know all about Him, for salvation comes through the Jews. But the time is coming— indeed it's here now—when true worshipers will worship the Father in spirit and in truth. The Father is looking for those who will worship Him that way. For God is Spirit, so those who worship Him must worship in spirit and in truth" (John 4:19-24 NLT).

Matthew 5:18—*"For truly I tell you, until heaven and earth disappear, not the smallest letter, not the least stroke of a pen, will by any means disappear from the Law until everything is accomplished"*— was fulfilled in 70 AD when the actual Temple of Jerusalem was destroyed. This one moment in history was so monumental because if "heaven and earth" (the old tabernacle) were not destroyed, then we would still be under the Mosaic Covenant. I can't explain to you in depth exactly everything that happened in 70 AD when Jerusalem was destroyed, because honestly, there are books upon books written about this very event. What I would suggest is for you to research further this matter yourself. At the end of this chapter, look for a book list complete with books that will take you deeper in your studies on this topic.

What I can tell you is that Nero led the Roman army in to destroy all of Israel, brutally and mercilessly. The Christians of that day fled to the mountains so that not even one Christian was recorded to have died in this horrific event. The happenings of this event are so disturbing and saddening that I cried when reading about them. The Temple was burned and then torn apart to where not even one brick stood upon the other. Jesus even prophesied of these events—eerily, very accurately:

> *Jesus came out from the temple and was going away when His disciples came up to point out the temple buildings to Him. And He said to them, "Do you not see all these things? Truly I say to you, not one stone here will be left upon another, which will not be torn down"* (Matthew 24:1-2 NASB).

The event I just described to you, I believe—and many scholars agree—is the event predicted in Hebrews 8:13, when it says that the Old Covenant is "soon to pass away"—so soon, in fact, that it happened only years later. The destruction of Jerusalem, along with the destruction of the Temple and temple system (all the genealogy scrolls were also destroyed, making it impossible to determine a Levitical priest system) was the removal of the Old Covenant system. Yes, there obviously was the attempt by man to recreate such a system; otherwise there would be no modern system of Judaism. I personally am thrilled that the Old Covenant system has passed away, although I do not take lightly the events of 70 AD. The people who stayed and were destroyed did so because they were hanging on to an old system, and they did not flee to the mountains as they could have. I'm very thankful for the New Covenant that Jesus established on new and better promises.

> *For this **reason Christ is the mediator of a new covenant**, that those who are called may receive the promised eternal inheritance—now that **He** [Jesus] **has died** as a ransom to set them free from the sins committed under the first covenant. In the case of a will, it is necessary **to prove the death of the one who made it**,*

*because a will is in force only when somebody has died; it never takes effect while the one who made it is living. This is why even the first covenant was not put into effect without blood. When Moses had proclaimed every command of the law to all the people, he took the blood of calves, together with water, scarlet wool and branches of hyssop, and sprinkled the scroll and all the people. He said, "This is the blood of the covenant, which God has commanded you to keep." In the same way, he sprinkled with the blood both the tabernacle and everything used in its ceremonies. In fact, the law requires that nearly everything be cleansed with blood, and without the shedding of blood there is no forgiveness. It was necessary, then, for the copies of the heavenly things to be purified with these sacrifices, but the heavenly things themselves with better sacrifices than these. **For Christ did not enter a sanctuary made with human hands that was only a copy of the true one**; He entered heaven itself, now to appear for us in God's presence. Nor did He enter heaven to offer Himself again and again, the way the high priest enters the Most Holy Place every year with blood that is not his own. Otherwise Christ would have had to suffer many times since the creation of the world. But He has appeared once for all at the culmination of the ages to do away with sin by the sacrifice of Himself* (Hebrews 9:15-26).

The people who are partakers of the New Covenant (that's us) are not bound to uphold the law that we read in Deuteronomy because the Old Covenant laws were laws for people who were partakers of the Mosaic Covenant (the Old Covenant). We are a part of the New Covenant, which we could also call the "Jesus Covenant." I say that because Moses was the mediator of the Mosaic Covenant, but Jesus is the mediator of the new and better covenant. So if Jesus is the mediator of the New Covenant, just how is it that we are able to partake in this covenant? I think these verses will answer that question:

> *For through the Law I died to the Law, so that I might live to God. I have been crucified with Christ; and it is no longer I who live, but Christ lives in me; and the life which I now live in the flesh I live by faith in the Son of God, who loved me and gave Himself up for me* (Galatians 2:19-20 NASB).

> *That they may all be one; even as You, Father, are in Me and I in You, that they also may be in Us, so that the world may believe that You sent Me. The glory which You have given Me I have given to them, that they may be one, just as We are one; I in them and You in Me,* [so] *that they may be perfected in* [brought to complete] *unity* (John 17:21-23 NASB).

Do you see it? The way we are able to partake in the New Covenant is to be found **in Christ**. In the New Covenant, by grace through faith we enter a glorious union with Jesus Christ. And how do we do that? It is by grace through faith that we are saved (see Eph. 2:8). By faith you entered into a covenantal relationship with God.

I've heard people describe how the law is broken up between moral law, judicial law, and ceremonial law, and that under the New Covenant, we're only bound to moral law. I have some major problems with that, the first of which being James 2:10, which I mentioned earlier:

> *For whoever keeps the whole law and yet stumbles at just one point is guilty of breaking all of it* (James 2:10).

What really boggles my mind about breaking the law into categories is that in all the Scripture the Mosaic Law is never ever categorized, so why now, all of a sudden, would it be? This is a modern-day practice in an attempt to decide which Old Covenant laws should apply to us today. You can't just make up classifications for the laws and then decide only certain ones apply to people who aren't even a part of that covenant. Furthermore, if you look through Deuteronomy and Leviticus, you'll see that those laws are not categorized. They are all mixed up. People have categorized them since then as an attempt to put Old Covenant laws on New Covenant believers.

In the New Covenant, there is actually a new law. Some people take the "moral laws" of the Old Covenant and add them to the commandments that Jesus gave in the New Testament, but for all the reasons I just explained, I believe that is the wrong approach. That doesn't mean we are lawless people, though. Jesus said many valuable and remarkable things. One of my favorite things to do when reading my Bible is to go read the Gospels so that I can imagine Jesus saying all those things. It makes me so happy to do that. Out of all the things Jesus said that is recorded in Scripture, He gave actual "commandments" pretty sparingly.

> *Carry each other's burdens, and in this way you will fulfill **the law of Christ** (Galatians 6:2).*

This "law of Christ" is mentioned here in Galatians. Jesus makes it pretty clear here what His NEW commandment was.

> *A new commandment I give to you, that you love one another: just as I have loved you, you also are to love one another (John 13:34 ESV).*

36

Think about this for a second. If someone entered a relationship with Jesus right now, today, and the only thing he or she knew was that Jesus has given this new commandment to love, that person could follow that one commandment and keep every commandment worth keeping, including all of the Ten Commandments. If you will follow the one commandment and keep that love relationship alive with God, you will be fulfilling every one of the Ten Commandments.

Love keeps me from stealing, killing, and cheating. Love keeps me from even having other "gods" cross my mind. Love fuels my good works so that I know I'm ministering out of an overflow.

This chapter is very important because it's a foundation for everything else I want to say. Because of Jesus, we are able to come to God in an amazing covenant relationship. No longer is God leading His people by a pillar of fire by night and smoke by day; rather, He's made His home within us so that we would have a blissful and glorious divine union with Him. He has literally written His law of love upon the fleshy tablets of our hearts. As you read the chapters to come, remember that the premise of everything I say is that you have a very personal relationship with God. He is with you. You can talk to Him, and He will speak to you.

Chapter 3

WOMEN IN LEADERSHIP

There are many amazing books out there that are about women in leadership. As you can tell, I'm somewhat of a book lover. I've dropped titles of other books all throughout this book. For me, something so powerful and freeing happened within my heart when I read Danny Silk's *Powerful and Free: Confronting the Glass Ceiling for Women in the Church.* I have loaned my copy out to anyone who has ever expressed interest in reading it, but I always have to explain why there are tear stains literally all the way through the book. What I read in that book set me free from forms of bondage I never even knew I was experiencing. I had been in bondage to lies that I had believed due to misinterpretation and misapplication of Scripture, but the more I read, the lighter I felt. If you have stressed over certain Scriptures because they appear at first glance to say that women shouldn't speak in church, then I want to tell you that the Bible has quite a great deal to say about women in leadership positions. Both in the Old Testament and in the New Testament, there are women that God directed into leadership positions, guiding both men and women.

Here's a really amazing tip for reading your Bible: if you come to a verse in your Bible that appears to contradict another verse in a different part of your Bible, then one thing is sure—**it deserves a closer look**. One of these verses is not being understood correctly because the Bible doesn't contradict itself. It's almost certain that if you find yourself in this situation, you're either misunderstanding one of the verses or you do not correctly understand the context of it. This is one little tool I use when reading and studying the Bible: when I run across one verse that seems to contradict another, that's my sign that I'm about to be doing some research to better understand both of these verses. One of the clearest and most obvious examples of this is the topic of women in leadership in the Bible. Did you know it's possible to build a case for almost anything by pulling Scripture verses out all over, putting them together, and leading people to conclusions? People have done it for years.

Many people say, "The Bible says it. I believe it. That settles it." That may sound nice, but what if the Bible said it, someone explained a misinterpreted version of it, and then you decided to stubbornly stand on what you *thought* it was saying, forever unmoving?

This absolutely does happen. I met a girl recently who believed that it was a sin to marry interracially because her whole life she had heard the story of the tower of Babel in Genesis 11, coupled with the verse in Second Corinthians 6:14 about not being unequally yoked, preached in a way that made it sound to her like God was opposed to people of different races marrying one another. It wasn't until later in her life, when she began to question these things and read the Scriptures for herself with an open mind to what God was really saying there, that she understood that she had been deceived.

During the time in the United States when slavery was legal, there were many people who argued FOR slavery, insisting that it was biblical. There were many brave people who were fighting for freedom, but there were many people who actually used Scripture to try to say that "since slavery is biblical, it should still be practiced as it is God's will." Hopefully that sounds completely insane to you now. Hopefully you're outraged at the thought that people would try to use Scripture to excuse something so terrible, but it really did happen.

> After 1830 there arose in the train of the "young politicians" of the era in the South a group of clerics who sought to defend slavery on scriptural and moral grounds. Their arguments effectively complemented the political theory so clearly enunciated by John C. Calhoun, the theory which became the foundation of the South's pro-slavery apologetic.[5]

> ...preachers, such as William Capers and William A. Smith, were composing biblical arguments in favor of slavery. These arguments defended slavery on several bases: first, that the Bible did not explicitly say slavery was wrong; second, that slavery actually seemed to be condoned by biblical writers like Paul; and third, that the institution of slavery was allowed by the government, and, since Christians are to submit to their governing authorities, they should have no problems with government-allowed slavery.[6]

As ridiculous and far-fetched as those examples might sound to some, others of you reading this may already be painfully aware that the same thing happens in churches all over the world. In many churches it is still common practice to use certain Scriptures to keep women out of leadership, to prevent them from talking in church, and ultimately to stand in the way of women whom God is calling into ministry. My point here is that for any behavior or lifestyle that exists under the sun, you can find people and "evidence" to justify their actions and form a case for what they want to believe. But if you have to pull verses out of context to prove your point, it's sort of like taking pieces from random and various jigsaw puzzles; trimming, gluing, and taping them to fit them together; and then trying to present the finished product. This isn't acceptable. I do believe progress is being made in the Church, but when I look around, I see there is still work to be done. I have a son and two daughters, and I want their lives to be better because of the work we are doing today. I want my ceiling to be their floor. I want the Kingdom to be further established than ever before because we refused to back down or be afraid of the enemy. This is possible, but it takes standing up for what is right in order to make a difference.

In this chapter, I want to show you how throughout history God has been appointing women to leadership roles and trying to lay a foundation for equality all along. When I'm done, I believe you will be absolutely shocked that all of this was always right in front of us in Scripture.

I realize that there are certain Scriptures in the Bible that seem confusing and limiting to women because of the context in which they've been taught over the years. This book's purpose is not to comb through each one of those verses. Books like Silk's *Powerful and Free*, Kris Vallotton's *Fashioned to Reign*, and other books explain those verses with proper historical context. If you want something that goes deeper into specifically explaining the verses that cause confusion, then I highly recommend that you get ahold of those two books. I know there are many more awesome resources out there, but I learned so much from Danny and Kris, and I want to set you up to go deeper if you read the information in my book and still want to know more. Although I will touch on some of these verses that cause confusion, my goal with this book is not to explain them all. There are other amazing books that do that, but I'm going in a different direction here.

GOD POSITIONING WOMEN TO LEAD— WOMEN IN LEADERSHIP

I want to be able to be somewhat of a storyteller in this section. I have stories to tell. I love these beautiful stories over which we often skip because many of us are "church folk" who've just sat through one too many "Sunday school lessons." Push aside every Sunday school lesson you've ever sat through, no matter how good or boring they might have been. I know you will value these stories because they're from the Bible, but they're also exciting tales of God's heart towards women. They are beautiful examples of God's desire for women to rule and reign as leaders and co-heirs. I believe with all my heart that God has called and is still calling women into leadership. The Bible tells of many things that have happened that weren't right or good, and I believe there are lessons to be learned from those things as well, but the stories I'll tell are stories that I believe prove to us that God is FOR women in leadership. He is not against women leading, and He Himself has positioned many a woman to do great things. There are plenty of strong, history-changing women leaders within the pages of our Bible. I don't believe the stories I'm about to tell are stories that you've heard a hundred times. I think they are probably stories that will make you gasp in surprise and then quickly grab your Bible (or, more likely, Google it to check on an online Bible) to double-check what I'm saying. So far in this book I have probably already shared at least one thing about which you were skeptical. That's okay. I will never ask you to just take my word for something when it comes to the weighty matter of teaching Scripture. I hope and pray that you will take Paul's advice in First Thessalonians 5:21 very seriously and test all things on which you hear pastors, teachers, and speakers teach. Test these things by the witness of the Holy Spirit who lives inside of you, but also test these things by the Word of God and research. Please double-check the things I say to you. That is my greatest desire—that people would question what they're told when it doesn't make sense and that they would learn how they themselves can also understand the Bible. It's good to have leaders in your life that you can trust, but it's not good to blindly believe anything someone says. That's the very thing I'm trying to get people NOT to do.

NOAH AND HIS WIFE

Noah was a man who was righteous and blameless before the Lord (see Gen. 6:9). He had a wife and three grown sons who were also married. Now God came to Noah because there were no other righteous and blameless people in the land, and He asked Noah to build a very large boat because God intended to flood the whole earth. God gave Noah specific measurements and instructions for the boat, and Scripture says that Noah did everything exactly as God asked of him (see Gen. 6:22; 7:5). Noah has one up on me in that area because I have a hard time even following the directions of a recipe. I normally just look at the ingredients and then wing the rest, taking my own creative liberties. My ark would have probably been bright turquoise with glitter paint, and God would have been there, shaking His head, asking Himself why He didn't find some-one who could follow directions better. But thankfully I haven't been called by God to build a boat because that was Noah's thing. Noah was the man for this job. A week before it started to rain, God gave Noah exact numbers of specific kinds of animals to take aboard. Apparently Noah really messed up and brought aboard cockroaches and spiders—a fail of epic proportions. I'm just kidding (kind of). Again, the Scriptures say that Noah did everything the Lord had asked of him. Good job, Noah (except for the roaches and spiders). The day came when the rains began to fall. Noah and his sons and all their wives went onto the great boat, and God closed the door behind them. The Bible states, *"That very day Noah had gone into the boat with his wife and his sons—Shem, Ham, and Japheth—**and their wives**"* (Gen. 7:13 NLT).

So they all went in the boat, God shut the door, and the rains poured down and eventually covered even the tallest mountain. I bet they all wished they had some episodes of *Downton Abbey* to watch while munching on corn chips, salsa, and guac during those boring rainy days. Or maybe not, but I'll let you read Scripture for yourself and decide. The floodwater covered the earth for 150 days. That's a long time to be on a boat with animals that poop. Noah began to realize that the floodwaters were receding, so he started to think about when it would be time to leave the boat. So far, God had been very specific about everything Noah was supposed to do. I would have been there trying to find out what kind of wood was on clearance, but God said, "gopher wood," and Noah used gopher wood. God said, "cubits," and Noah measured the right measurements in cubits. So when it came time to leave the boat, God again had specific instructions:

> *Then God said to Noah, "Leave the boat, all of you—* ***you and your wife, and your sons and their wives"*** (Genesis 8:15-16 NLT).

Do you see what I see? You might not see it right off the bat, so let me hone in a little closer so that you can take notice of something that might SEEM insignificant after we've sat through the same darn Sunday school story over and over again. But in light of how SPE-CIFIC God was with Noah throughout this whole ordeal, I don't think any instructions can be ignored. Noah was a man of details. And I recognize that because although I don't follow directions very well, I'm awesome at giving directions. Oh, I can tell somebody what to do, all right. And I believe God was being specific on PURPOSE. Look at this:

Going on the boat, the Bible states:

> *"That very day Noah had gone into the boat with his wife and his sons—Shem, Ham, and Japheth—**and their wives**"* (Genesis 7:13 NLT).

Coming off the boat, God has specific instructions:

> *"Then God said to Noah, 'Leave the boat, all of you— **you and your wife, and your sons and their wives'"*** (Genesis 8:15-16 NLT).

When Noah went on the boat, he and his sons went on, and their wives followed behind them. When they left the boat, God gave precise instructions about how they were to leave the ark. He says for them to leave the boat, all of them, like this: *"...you and your wife... your sons and their wives"* (Gen. 8:16). I find this extremely interesting, and could we possibly draw the conclusion that God was attempting to set forth a new precedent of equality? I think so. I really do. According to Scripture it appears that again Noah obeyed the Lord: *"Noah, his wife, and his sons and their wives left the boat"* (Gen. 8:18 NLT).

I love this story. You can and should read the whole thing with a close eye on all the details. I bet by the time you're finished reading you find at least one thing that makes you say, "Hey, this isn't like how they retold this story to me in kid's church/Sunday school!" It's pretty awesome when we read God's Word with new eyes and an open mind to what He's trying to say to us. You can find the whole story in Genesis 5:32–10:1.

RUTH AND BOAZ

Ruth was the daughter-in-law of Naomi. Sadly, Naomi's husband and son (Ruth's husband) lost their lives in battle. Ruth was so faithful to Naomi that she refused to leave or abandon her. Naomi realized that Ruth was determined to remain loyal to her, and she decided to take Ruth back with her to her hometown of Bethlehem. They moved back to Bethlehem together, and upon arriving, Ruth suggested to Naomi that she go and glean at one of the local fields. Naomi approved, and while gleaning wheat at a local field, Ruth met Boaz. Boaz was very kind to her and told her to come back the next day. Boaz then instructed his workers to make sure they leave behind plenty of wheat for her, and even drop plenty, to make it easier on Ruth. At lunchtime, Boaz called Ruth over to eat of his bread.

When Ruth went home, she showed Naomi all that she gathered that day. Naomi was so impressed that she asked Ruth where in the world she went to gather that much. When Ruth told her that she had gone to the fields of Boaz, Naomi was delighted and insisted that Ruth go back the next day, which Ruth continued to do throughout the entire barley harvest season.

The day came when Naomi told Ruth to go bathe, put on her best clothes, and go to Boaz. The thing that Naomi asked of Ruth was quite scandalous, actually. She specifically told Ruth to wait until Boaz had finished eating and drinking, and then when he lies down, Ruth should go lay at his feet and do whatever he says. Then again, Ruth and Naomi both knew Boaz's character. They knew he was a man of honor. Ruth did as Naomi told her, except when she lay on his feet, she told Boaz, *"Spread the corner of your covering over me, for you are my family redeemer"* (Ruth 3:9 NLT). In modern-day lingo, that would be the equivalence of Ruth asking Boaz to marry her. Boaz was honored that Ruth would come to him. He realized she was young and beautiful and that she could have sought after younger men. He let her know there was a closer relative that would rightfully be her kinsman redeemer so he would go to him first to see if he wanted to take Ruth as his wife. After the other man declined, Boaz did take Ruth as his wife, and they had a beautiful baby boy for Naomi to cuddle and love.

What an amazing story of a woman taking the lead. She didn't wait around for Boaz to ask her for her hand in marriage. She did as Naomi said, and their story unfolded beautifully. If anything, this should tell us that many of the customs we have today don't really line up with the Bible. I can't even count how many times I've been told that "the Bible says a woman shouldn't pursue a man," yet here we have a beautiful story, in the lineage of Jesus, where just such a situation takes place. Obviously there was a lot of wisdom involved. Neither Ruth nor Naomi was being reckless. There was a history here where they knew the integrity of Boaz. Sure, there may have been some risk involved here, but I believe when it comes down to it, the plan was from the Lord.

PHOEBE AND JUNIA—NEW COVENANT WOMEN LEADERS

In the New Testament, included in our Scripture that we now call the Bible are letters from someone we know as the Apostle Paul. In one of these letters, I find something very curious and notable. Now before I jump into what I find so amazeballs (that's a word I may or may not have coined that we should just all accept into normal and permissible vocabulary) in one of these letters, I should give you some background information about Paul. Now Paul is sometimes talked about like he was some kind of woman hater because people take out of context things Paul said in other letters he wrote, but I don't think Paul was a woman hater at all. I think Paul was all for empowering and honoring women leaders of character, and you'll see that in a second. Remember earlier in the book when I mentioned what to do if you have two verses that seem to be in conflict with one another? Well, this applies here, especially when the same guy who said women have to be silent in church starts giving recognition to a woman deacon and apostle. It leaves you asking yourself, "Come on, Paul, are you for women in leadership or not?" At least I hope it does. Paul wasn't against women speaking in church, otherwise he wouldn't have praised a woman deacon and a woman apostle in one of his other letters.

So Paul, in this letter, is giving recognition, honor, and thanks to different people. He also commends a woman named Phoebe. She is actually the first person named in the letter, and she is mentioned as a deacon at a church. The very next people referenced are a couple, Andronicus and Junia, who are noted as outstanding among the apostles.

> Greet Andronicus and Junia, my fellow Jews who have been in prison with me. They are outstanding among the apostles, and they were in Christ before I was (Romans 16:7).

> I commend to you our sister Phoebe, a deacon of the church in Cenchreae. I ask you to receive her in the Lord in a way worthy of His people and to give her any help

she may need from you, for she has been the benefactor of many people, including me. Greet Priscilla and Aquila, my co-workers in Christ Jesus. They risked their lives for me. Not only I but all the churches of the Gentiles are grateful to them. Greet also the church that meets at their house (Romans 16:1-5).

There are so many other stories of God commissioning women to leadership in the Bible that I could have listed here, but I specifically chose these, partially because they are some of my favorites but mainly because they show a side of femininity that strokes against the grain of what we are programmed as a culture to believe about women. I'm proposing to you that in the story of Noah, God was establishing a beautiful picture of equality. In the story of Ruth and Boaz, we find two women who are strong and resourceful and not afraid to make the first move. In the letters that Paul wrote, we learn that he wasn't a male chauvinist and that he wasn't ashamed to promote and exhort women in leadership positions. I love these stories. They are so rich and beautiful. My nanny used to tell me, "The Word of God is the most beautiful book you'll ever read. If you want adventure, it's in there. If you want romance, it's in there. If you want mystery and scandal, it's in there too." I tend to agree. What a beautiful book.

FAMILY AND MINISTRY/LEADERSHIP

Family and ministry can sometimes be tricky to balance. It can often be tempting to chase after building a ministry and put your family on the back burner. Whether you are a man or a woman reading, know this: family is your first ministry. If you are the next Billy Graham but you failed to be a lover to your spouse and a parent to your kids, that is not success. All through the New Testament, we read that married leaders were first required to show faithfulness at home before they could even be considered for leadership in the Church. We don't need to get this twisted. We can't get in our heads that we must neglect our families in order to do all that God has called us to do. In reality, they (your family) are a huge part of what God has called you to do. That doesn't mean that God hasn't also called you into ministry or called you to run a huge, successful business. It just means that our families must always be put before ministry.

This is why I left you in Crete, so that you might put what remained into order, and appoint elders in every town as I directed you—if anyone is above reproach, the husband of one wife, and his children are believers and not open to the charge of debauchery or insubordination. For an overseer, as God's steward, must be above reproach. He must not be arrogant or quick-tempered or a drunkard or violent or greedy for gain, but hospitable, a lover of good, self-controlled, upright, holy, and disciplined. He must hold firm to the trustworthy word as taught, so that he may be able to give instruction in sound doctrine and also to rebuke those who contradict it (Titus 1:5-9 ESV).

The saying is trustworthy: If anyone aspires to the office of overseer, he desires a noble task. Therefore an overseer must be above reproach, the husband of one wife, sober-minded, self-controlled, respectable, hospitable, able to teach, not a drunkard, not violent but gentle, not quarrelsome, not a lover of money. He must manage his own household well, with all dignity keeping his children submissive, for if someone does not know how to manage

his own household, how will he care for God's church?
(1 Timothy 3:1-5 ESV).

Just because women are not specified in these passages of Scripture doesn't mean that women can't also be leaders in ministry. Remember, previously I just listed many women who held positions of leadership within the pages of our Bible.

Women in leadership positions are nothing new. All throughout the pages of our Bibles we see women who were leading, clearly with the approval of God. We see God establishing a basis for equality, and we see Him equipping women to rule and reign. In later chapters, I have included even more stories from Scripture that may surprise you and lure you into the beauty and bliss of the Bible.

For further information on the events of 70 AD, consult the following works:

- Jonathan Welton's *Raptureless* (Extended Edition)

- David Chilton's *The Days of Vengeance: An Exposition of the Book of Revelation*

- Kenneth L. Gentry Jr.'s *Before Jerusalem Fell: During the Book of Revelation*

- Harold R. Eberle and Martin Trench's *Victorious Eschatology*

Chapter 4

BEAUTY, CONFIDENCE, AND AUTHENTICITY

"Beauty is in the eye of the beholder," I've heard people say. I've come to believe that a more accurate phrase would be that "beauty is in the eye of the Creator." It's funny because depending on what part of the world in which you grew up, different cultures have different ideas and standards of what beauty is. Because a woman is born and raised in the United States she will likely have different ideas about what makes a woman beautiful. She will likely have standards of beauty that fit the cultural norm of the society in which she grew up. Whatever society deems beautiful, more than likely, most people will desire to fit that and the majority of girls will hope to look like that. Not everyone strives for mainstream beauty, and I believe part of God's Feminist Movement is awakening within the hearts of His people a desire to be completely authentic. I want to propose to you that you were born to disrupt the culture in whatever part of the world you happen to live. I believe we are all about to infiltrate our culture with the culture of heaven. Since we are ambassadors for the Kingdom of Heaven and the Kingdom of Heaven is within us, I believe we are called to release the heart of the Kingdom of God into our cultures (see 2 Cor. 5:20; Luke 17:21). That is disrupting culture. If you traveled the world, you would find that different cultures have their own standards of beauty. For example, I remember reading, as a child, a magazine article about a remote tribe whose culture found a long slender neck to be an attractive feature on a person. But there are certainly other cultures in the world that do not place the same value on this physical characteristic. But what is the cultural norm in the Kingdom of Heaven? What defines true beauty? Let's talk more about this.

My mom always taught me to say, "Thank you" when someone pays me a compliment, so anytime anyone has ever told me that I'm beautiful or pretty, I would always say, "Thank you." But there was a point in my life when I said, "Thank you" only with my mouth while my mind screamed, "NO YOU'RE NOT! They are wrong! It was just a good angle! They are just being polite." In no way did I believe what they said. Immediately I would begin to think of all the things that made me not pretty, in my opinion. I fantasized about everything from having liposuction to having a nose job, dental reconstructive surgery, or even a tummy tuck. I didn't say those things out loud to anyone else very often, but they still had an impact on those around me. I was a leader in the church at this time—and a youth pastor at that—and so plenty of young women looked up to me. I didn't dare say how much I hated my appearance, but I know that my lack of love for myself kept me from loving others freely as well. I sometimes wish I could go back and speak with all my girls at the first church we ever pastored so that I could share my heart on beauty now. The Father has changed my perspective so much since those days! I wish I could share my story with them so that they would know what I was going through on the inside and also so that they too can walk in the freedom that God has led me into, the freedom to love myself. Who knows, maybe this book is a way to get that message in their hands. Let me take you on this walk to freedom, confidence, and the ability to love yourself. Here, take my hand.

In the fall of 2010, I began the discovery journey of a lifetime. This was a very special spiritual journey for me, although if you had asked me at the time, I would have called it a weight-loss journey. I had no idea God wanted to use my vanity to do anything spiritual, to bring me to a greater level of freedom. I was just trying to get rid of all the fat that I hated so much. I thought it would improve my life and help me accept my own reflection in the mirror. God had other plans, though. He took me on a wild ride, opening my eyes to my self-worth and beauty like never before. I had no idea what kind of a ride He was about to take me on. I had simply decided to try to lose some weight. After having three kids, I had kept on a little extra weight and found myself slightly overweight. I was so grossed out by my appearance. I really did hate the way I looked. I bought myself one of those Spanx control top girdles that look like high-rise bicycle shorts to start wearing underneath my clothes. They would make my stomach cramp so terribly after a few hours of wearing them, but I would wear them anyways. Right after I started wearing them a few people asked me if I had lost weight. I remember how disgusted I felt. I was cheating, and even their compliments reminded me that I was "fat." It was like I was torturing myself with those things just to try to lose my muffin top, but still, even when I would wear one I would look in the mirror and all I could do was pick myself apart with criticism.

I had had three cesarean sections by this point, and the first one was an emergency c-section, so when I would look in the mirror I would look at that scar with loathing. Every one else I knew who had had a c-section had a cute little horizontal, "bikini cut" incision, but my scar is vertical. I thought it looked a lot like a butt crack because of the little bit of extra weight I was carrying. I know, TMI, but I'm trying to keep it real with you here so you'll know how terrible my self-image had become at this time. One Sunday morning after church, I heard two ladies talking about meeting in the children's ministry room to work out every day using a workout program one of them had ordered off of television. The room was carpeted and had a huge projector screen so it was a perfect fit. The workouts were super intense. It was extremely hard at first, but I stuck with it and got pretty good at it. The problem was that according to the scale, with which I was obsessed at the time, I wasn't losing anything. It was pretty frustrating for me as I went through the whole ninety days of the program without seeing but about five pounds go. Honestly, I had been expecting a loss greater than that, but little did I know that something very amazing, surprising, and life-changing was about to happen.

I want to take a second to reiterate something here before I launch into the rest of this story: this is an extremely unhealthy attitude about self-image that I'm describing here. This is a part of my story, and God worked this together for good. I had no idea that the root of my self-hatred was not my weight. I had no idea at the time that this was a terribly unhealthy way to look at my body. I had objectified my own body and decided that my self-worth was determined by my appearance. God used my interest in weight loss to remove the scales from my eyes and lead me into a deeper level of intimacy with Him.

That year, in January, our entire church did a collective fast. Now, in the Bible, you can read about fasting with only water, or even fasting where the person doesn't eat anything, but for this particular fast I decided to do what people call a "Daniel Fast." There are many other books you could read if you want to know more, but the premise is that in Daniel 1, it is said that Daniel and his men would not eat the food being served to them because it had been offered to the idols as a sacrifice. Daniel felt conviction in his heart about this, and so he refused to partake of the food. Instead, he asked them to feed him and his men only vegetables, fruit, and water. They agreed to Daniel's request to do this but were skeptical. To everyone's surprise, Daniel and his men were the fastest and strongest of all the men (see Dan. 1:8-15). I decided that the way I would participate in this collective fast was by doing what people call a Daniel Fast. I also determined that I did not want to give up working out. It had been so hard to get back in shape that I did not want to start all over at the end of the twenty-one-day fast.

A couple of days into the fast, I was absolutely astonished to find that pounds of fat were literally melting right off of me. After the withdrawal headaches and the other undesirable detoxification side effects wore off (this took about a week), I felt like thirty million bucks. I couldn't believe how amazing I felt and how much energy I had, but even more than that, I couldn't believe that after all this time of working out with no results, I had finally had a breakthrough. During the fast I lost a considerable amount of weight.

Toward the end of the fast, I came to the conclusion that I did not want to go back to eating the way I always had. I knew that I needed to find out what it was about the fast that made me feel so amazing. I had thought that it possibly was that I had cut back on calories. But after thinking about it, that didn't make sense to me because even while on the fast I practically ate truckloads. My caloric intake was probably still around the same as before the fast so I suspected that the key to my sudden weight loss wasn't calorie restriction. It had to be something else.

This led me to do some digging around. I started researching and stumbled upon what is widely known as a concept called "clean eating." Many people have probably heard about this by now, but I will briefly describe it for you. This is no nutrition book, but I know if I mention it without explaining a little, it's going to leave a lot of people with a lot of questions. Basically, the Creator fashioned our bodies to need fuel to survive. The Creator also made food for us to eat for nourishment. (This Creator character sounds kind of clever.) It is my belief that if we eat the foods that God created in as close to a natural state as possible, then our bodies will function properly and healthfully. For many people that will result in weight loss. Our bodies were not designed to eat man-made chemicals, artificial coloring and flavoring, preservatives, and processed junk food out of packages and boxes. These kinds of synthetics are in packaged food, and they are foreign and unrecognizable to our bodies. Remember, the Creator made our bodies with HIS food in mind, not the lab experiments that you will find on the shelves of grocery stores. Your body doesn't recognize that stuff, and it stores it as fat. This is why many people are seriously depriving themselves of calories by drinking diet soda, eating sugar-free and reduced calorie/reduced fat foods, yet seeing little to no results. This is EXACTLY the frustration I was experiencing all those years ago. Without even realizing what I was doing, the Daniel Fast that I did sent my body into a fat burning frenzy merely because I quit ingesting chemicals, preservatives, refined sugar, flour, sodas, and other unnatural, packaged junk food. Researching the clean-eating concept was so beneficial for me, because in doing this I learned that healthy fats like nuts, avocado, olive oil, and animal fats are vital to our brain health. It contradicts the mainstream nutritional theories of our American society, but healthy fats do NOT make people fat. Full-fat, raw dairy from grass-fed cows became my preference when it came to milk consumption (like I said, this is no nutrition book, and you're more than free to disagree with me). The theory behind this is very simple: when we eat foods in the natural state, we are eating them the way God intended for us to eat them. Since He created our bodies, I believe He knows better than anyone how we should nourish this amazingly intricate machine we call a body.

I'm not endorsing weight loss for the sake of fulfilling the mainstream media's idea of attractiveness, nor would I ever suggest that any one particular body type is healthy. I just think it is important for me to say this on the record: You are beautiful, no matter what size you are. I think it is a bad idea to crash diet, take diet pills, starve yourself, or use any other extreme or unhealthy means of weight loss. At the root of those methods is self-hatred, and I've been there.

During the Daniel Fast, specifically around week two, I realized that I had been doing something I call "emotional eating." I had been using food to soothe myself any time I was feeling hurt, angry, or depressed. I realized that I had not been turning to my relationship with Jesus whenever life's trials would strike. Instead, I was turning to my comfort junk foods. God started showing me how much this grieved His heart. He used that fast to open my eyes to how dependent I had become on the foods that I loved and how much I had been pushing God away when I was hurt. In short, I was allowing food to fulfill a need in my life that only God was meant to fulfill. This was just the first epiphany of this journey. It rocked me to the core. When I realized what I had been doing, I feel like something just clicked. I realized that God could offer me something that even the most decadent chocolate ice cream with caramel swirls couldn't: true comfort and peace. When I realized this, I had the most amazing visual pop into my head. (Sometimes something really cool will happen to me: I will have this experience with God where He gives me a video that shines up on the screen of my imagination. The Bible calls this a vision.) So God gave me one of these mental videos. There I was, angry, hurt, and feeling betrayed. I was crying and wishing that someone cared about the pain I was going through. "Forget this!" I thought, as I decided to sweep my feelings under the rug and instead grab some cookies and milk. "Nothing cheers me up quite like cookies and milk," I thought. And there was Jesus. He was sitting there in my living room, and it appeared that He was trying to get my attention. I didn't pay Him any mind at first because I was really busy having a temper tantrum/pity party. Suddenly I noticed Him sitting there in my recliner in my living room, and I felt this overwhelming longing to climb into His lap. The food and other comforts didn't seem quite so comforting as I saw Him sitting there, beckoning me over. I rushed over to Him and climbed up in His lap. He wrapped His arms around me, and I just began to cry and cry on His shoulder. There I was, in this vision, sobbing on His shoulder, and suddenly this velvety, warm feeling of peace washed over me. I felt fulfilled. I felt the same feeling you get halfway through downing a glass of ice water after mowing the lawn on a summer day in the Texas heat: refreshment. I felt like I had found a long-lost friend, even though I had been saved for several years. I had just not known Him at this level. Until this point I hadn't had a revelation of God as this very close and intimate friend who would come into my living room to sit in my recliner, pull me into His lap, and allow me to cry on His shoulder. I realized then that God was telling me that if I would turn to Him in those times of betrayal, hurt, stress, and tragedy, He would be there for me, no matter how deep the pain. He's not just a God that is far removed from His creation. God was showing me that He wanted to be my very best friend. He was showing me that He could give me something that emotional eating would never in a million years be able to give me. I had developed a kind of sick relationship with food where it met a deep hunger within me, but God was showing me that one contributing factor to my self-hatred was that I was turning to food to fulfill a need inside of me that only He could fulfill. Obviously, the food wasn't really getting to the core of my pain, but in that moment Jesus touched that throbbing pain and soothed it in an instant.

Popular culture, society, and the enemy have this way of pushing their opinion of beauty on us, and I disagree with that. Dressing provocatively doesn't make a woman beautiful. Being trendy and on the cutting edge of fashion doesn't make a woman beautiful. Even the way a lady carries herself with dignity and grace isn't what makes her beautiful. You are beautiful because God created you. When God created you, He made no mistake. He didn't accidentally give you freckles. I like to imagine Him giving you freckles, stepping back with a proud Papa smile, and saying, "That's good." He didn't accidentally make your hair brown. He carefully and meticulously knitted you together before you were even born. He put thought into what He would make you look and sound like and what would make up the essence of who you are. When you hate on yourself, you are telling God that what He made isn't good enough.

ACTIVATION

Do yourself a favor and walk to a mirror. Look yourself square in the eye and tell yourself that the King of this universe designed you. He made you, He loves you, and HE says you're BEAUTIFUL. Who will you believe? Him or society? Now do yourself another favor and throw out all those magazines that shove the anorexic/skinny/ripped/ voluptuous superstars down your throat with the label of "beautiful" slapped all over them. They don't have the authority to define beautiful. You are not that girl in the magazine and you will never be (but that is not a bad thing). Beauty has many faces. Stop looking at the ladies you know, wishing you could just be as thin/tall/graceful/ fashionable as them. YOU are beautiful, unique, quirky, and ADORED. Jesus loves you with a love that is unfathomable. Quench your thirst with HIS love because then you will thirst no more.

I felt very led to write this because I have many young lady friends, and I never want to be misunderstood. The number one thing I pray you would realize is that if you can't love yourself at 220 pounds, you'll never love yourself at 120 pounds. You'll just find something else to hate about yourself. You need a revelation of who you are to Jesus. At any size, you are His beloved. Never forget that. That alone will cause you to begin to care for the health of your body because you are a temple of the Holy Spirit. You were called and created to be a move of God in the earth. You have one life ahead of you to change the world for the better. You want to make the most of your years here in this life by taking care of your health. You were destined to have longevity, good health, and stamina in ministry. Allow me to reiterate something because I want to drive this point home. Before you ever try to change your appearance, lose weight, or anything, you need to know this:

If you can't love yourself at 220 pounds, you won't be able to love yourself at 120 pounds.

The reason why this is true is that your appearance isn't the reason you can't love yourself. You may have been telling yourself, "If I could just tone up my abs a little, then I would be pleased with who I am," "If I could just lose ten pounds, then I would be content," or, "If I could just afford the kind of clothes I really want, then I know I would be confident." But those are all lies. After you could afford the wardrobe of your dreams, you would find something else just outside of your reach off of which to base your happiness. The truth is that with this kind of mindset, you'll always be unhappy, discontented, and unsatisfied with who you are as a person. You have to get rid of this mindset for good. Now I'm not saying you will be able to rid yourself of this mindset once and for all, never to be tempted ever again, **instantly**. What happens is that when you come to the awakening that I'm hoping this book brings you to, you will feel so pumped and so free from those toxic mindsets of self-hatred. But the truth of the matter is that one day later down the road when someone says something rude about your appearance, some kid asks you when your baby is due but you're not pregnant, or your grandpa tells you you're too skinny and he's worried you're sick (don't ask me how I know this will happen or where I got these very realistic-sounding examples), it will be very tempting to pick back up those toxic ways of thinking and start beating yourself up. Don't do that. You are stepping into this freedom, and though you will have days where you don't feel like a sassy, little, gorgeous love muffin, don't you dare go back to loathing yourself. You are beautiful, and no high-humidity-induced crazy hair day can change that. That's because your beauty was never dependent on that in the first place. Your beauty has always come from the fact that you are a creation of the Creator.

Some time after God opened my eyes to my problem with emotional eating, I had a very powerful dream:

I'm sitting in my kitchen when my oldest child Joseph comes into the room with this painting. "Mom!" he exclaims proudly. "Look at this." He is holding a canvas in his hands; he is clearly excited, and on the canvas is a painting that he made especially for his mommy. I look at the painting that his chubby little hands are holding and begin to criticize and pick it apart. "I don't like the color green. There's too much green in it. It doesn't match any room in my house. I don't know where I'll put it. Maybe I can change it or we can paint over it in order to improve it and make it more bearable."

With each insult, I see his face fall slightly, and then even more, as I ridicule the artwork that he had worked so hard to create for me.

I woke up from that dream and sat straight up in bed. Now I wasn't skilled or trained in dream interpretation at all back then (not that I'm an expert now or anything), but my mind was spinning. I wondered why I was so mean. That was totally out of character. I never would have responded to one of my children like that in real life, but then God dropped a metaphorical bomb in my lap. In the dream, I represented God. Joseph represented God's children, specifically myself during this season. God was trying to show me that we are His masterpiece. I had no problem admiring a gorgeous landscape as a beautiful part of God's creation, but at the time I had great difficulty with seeing myself as part of God's beautiful creation. He gave me this dream partly so I could understand how He feels when I pick myself apart with harsh criticism. This dream deeply impacted me and opened my eyes. It also helped me realize that God determines what is beautiful. When we finally realize that, we can see the beauty in anyone we meet.

What makes a woman beautiful isn't whether or not she can pull off the latest fashion trends. It also isn't a freshly toned body. It's because she is one of God's masterpieces. She is created by God and loved by God. Her beauty isn't dependent on the aesthetic standards of society. Society doesn't have the authority to decide who is beautiful. Neither does popular culture. Neither do I, nor do haters on the Internet. God is the Creator. He made you, and He calls you beautiful. That is where true confidence and self-love comes from.

Let me free you from a little Christian myth that you may have, like me, believed your whole life: Loving yourself is not a bad thing. Loving yourself is necessary. Loving yourself is the key step to loving others.

> *Hearing that Jesus had silenced the Sadducees, the Pharisees got together. One of them, an expert in the law, tested Him with this question: "Teacher, which is the greatest commandment in the Law?" Jesus replied: "'Love the Lord your God with all your heart and with all your soul and with all your mind.' This is the first and greatest commandment. And the second is like it: 'Love your neighbor as yourself.' All the Law and the Prophets hang on these two commandments"* (Matthew 22:34-40).

Here's what I'm not trying to say here: I'm not trying to say that God gave a third commandment to love ourselves, but I do think that a natural conclusion here is that in order to have a healthy love for others, we first must love ourselves.

It's vital for us to realize that God loves us and to receive His love. It's extremely important that we learn to love ourselves, but spiritual maturity is realizing that just as much as God's heart passionately loves and accepts US, He loves others as well. Here's something to think about: God desperately and fervently loves the person you dislike the most in the world. The most despicable person in the world is still loved by God. That person may have committed heinous crimes against humanity, and you can be assured that they grieved God's heart and He didn't agree with or love their choices. But He absolutely, without a doubt, loves all of humanity. I don't know about you, but that really puts life in perspective for me. If God loves a person, surely I can look at him or her with His eyes and see something worth loving. Surely I can look at that person and find beauty.

At the beginning of the year 2015, I made the New Year's resolution to be unapologetically myself. What does that mean? Well, I just decided I wanted to be myself. I decided I wanted to like what I like, wear what makes me feel confident and beautiful, laugh at the things I find funny until I snort, and just stop living for other people...without any shred of guilt. I realized right away that subconsciously I had been living my life for the approval of other people. I had made actual life choices based off of whether or not other people would be offended.

I'm not talking about living a self-serving life here. I'm talking about embracing who God created you to be and living that out without apologizing to everyone all the time for loving folk music, unicorns, and root beer floats. God created you with likes and dislikes. You have a unique taste, whether it be in fashion, painting, interior design, creating totally funky and awesome outfits, makeup, art, or writing. You don't have to change who you are in order to be liked by others.

> *"If you don't live by the praise of men,*
> *you won't die by their criticism."*
> —BILL JOHNSON

You owe it to the world to be yourself. There is a move of God in the earth that only you can release. Have you ever seen a water hose with kinks in it? It's like you're a water hose, and the water flowing through you is God's glory. Those kinks in the water hose are obstructions. They are keeping the water from flowing through as strongly as it could. Those kinks represent people who can't embrace who they are. They can't accept who God has created them to be so they're busy trying to be like someone else. They are busy trying to change themselves or attempting to put forth an image of themselves that they think people will like more. When you just decide to be yourself, it's like you're going down that hose, unkinking all those kinks. And as you embrace who God created you to be, you're going to release His glory in the earth in that very special and unique way that only you can.

I want to be very clear here that I'm not encouraging people to embrace sinful or destructive behavior as a part of how God created you. If you have a habit of being very rude and mean to other people, God did not make you that way. I don't point this out to bring you condemnation but rather to point out the truth. God has set us free from being slaves to sin. If you are struggling with being financially responsible or struggling with staying faithful to your spouse, that is not a part of your identity, and I'm not trying to encourage you to accept sin as "just the way God made you." That's something Jesus paid a great price to set you free from, so I wouldn't want to be a part of someone's justification of ungodly behavior. That's not something He wants you to embrace as a part of who you are.

An example of this from my life is my loudness. Being loud isn't a bad thing. I'm naturally a very loud person. I have no problem projecting my voice across a room, and my laugh can range anywhere from a loud belly laugh—"hahahahaha"—to the loudest, most uncontrollable snort in the room. The more excited or passionate I get about something, the louder I will probably get. When I try to talk on my phone in stores, like when I'm grocery shopping, I have to be really careful about the volume of my voice, especially when talking about sensitive things. There's nothing really wrong with being loud, but here's the thing: when I get mad, the first thing that I do is to start to get really loud, which often leads to yelling. I'm actually working on this, and I've matured so much over the years in this area. Yelling isn't a sin, but there's kind of a problem with just yelling at people when they make you mad. My husband is pretty sensitive to this, and he was one of the first people to point out to me that I had this problem. My first response to him was, "Well, I'm just a loud person. I've always been loud." I mean, I didn't come right out and say it, but my thought was, "This is just the way I am, so deal with it." God began to deal with my heart as I came around to the idea that it was hurting my relationship with the guy I love more than anything and that I was being a big loudmouth, yelling at him instead of trying to take the time to explain myself rationally. You're free because Christ set you free, but you're not free to hurt others. You're free to set other people free.

> *It was for freedom that Christ set us free...* (Galatians 5:1 NASB).

> *You, my brothers and sisters, were called to be free. But do not use your freedom to indulge the flesh; rather, serve one another humbly in love. For the entire law is fulfilled in keeping this one command: "Love your neighbor as yourself"* (Galatians 5:13-14).

How did I get to the point where I began to care more about being authentic than about pleasing other people? Honestly, I've always wanted to be well-liked. I'm not ashamed to admit that. And to be really and completely honest with you right now, I still really enjoy being well-liked…. But here's the deal: the way I live my life and the choices I make are ultimately between me and God and my immediate family. Every one of us would be the best versions of our self if we just learned to love ourselves, see ourselves through God's eyes, and stop living for the approval of other people.

So how's this going for me? Gosh…I'm liberated! I went out and got a tattoo I've wanted for years, I feel more beautiful and confident than ever before, and I feel that my relationship with God has flourished like a beautiful flower. You see, I found that I can't live for the approval of others and still be living for God. It's like I would hear what I wanted to hear, and when I wanted to make the choices that I believed I would be well liked for, subconsciously I was putting God's opinion (on whatever the matter was at hand) on the back burner. I didn't realize I was doing that until I purposely started giving myself permission to live only for His approval.

There will always be someone who doesn't like you. You have nothing to lose by being authentic. Think about a time when you felt like you kind of compromised who you are in order to please someone. It doesn't matter if it was back in high school when you dressed a certain style to please others, pretended to have so much more in common with someone because you wanted to be accepted, or maybe just held back from doing something truly awesome because you were afraid of what people would have to say about your choices. There were still people who didn't like you. Even though you made slightly different choices to keep from upsetting certain people, or in order to please certain people, there were still people who didn't like your choices or just didn't like you. Wouldn't it have been so much easier to just have been yourself? Sure, there will always be people who don't like you, but you won't be any worse off than you were when you weren't being true to yourself. Plus, life will be easier and more fulfilling because you're letting down the façade and embracing who you truly are. When you're you, you free others to be authentic. Also, when you embrace who you are, you will begin to accept others for who they are as well. That's a huge sign of maturity—to begin to appreciate and accept people who are very different than you.

As a mom, one of the things I really want my children to understand is that God loves them so much. It's really important for these little guys to know how loved they are by God. It's absolutely crucial. But there comes a point when they move beyond just knowing that God loves THEM to acknowledging and realizing that God loves others with that same intensity. When we really get that, it changes how we treat others.

There is a move of God in the earth that only you can fulfill; this is absolutely true. There is also a move of God in the earth for each person. We must never become so self-absorbed that we are fooled into thinking that our "calling" or "destiny" is more important than someone else's. I've seen this too many times to count. There are so many different callings in the Kingdom. Advancing the Kingdom looks different from person to person. Here's something I've noticed over the years: within the Church (and even in a secular environment), people have a tendency to segregate themselves into groups of like-minded people.

I'm going to use a slightly over-exaggerated scenario involving the Church. Over here we have the academic, intellectual camp of individuals who are clutching their Greek lexicons, studying the root words. They like reason. For them, things need to make sense, and a lot of hokey pokey might not be tolerated. Emotionalism doesn't have a lot of room over here in this camp, so if you have a case to build for, let's say, a supernatural encounter with God, then you'll need to first build your case with similar experiences in Scripture.

Moving along, we have another camp down the road a little ways. This camp is the prophetic intercessor, seer camp. These guys are running down the aisles of the church with their ribbons and tambourines, as one after the other share their prophetic visions of angels, speak in tongues, give a word of knowledge, and then interpret each other's dreams using only song and dance.

I'm not going to describe any more "camps." This is enough to help you see what I've seen over the years. If one of these academic, intellectual guys comes over here to the prophetic camp, he won't likely be well received—because he thinks differently than they do. He's trying to be the voice of reason and explain that in the Bible, there is this verse over here about such and such. Here's the kicker: **these two groups of people need each other.** The last thing they need is to be so far detached from one another that they can't learn from one another. They bring balance to each other. Now I know I exaggerated these two camps a little. I used extreme examples to drive my point home, but we probably all can think of slightly less extreme real-life examples where groups of people who are similar sort of create their own small group and don't really like to get outside of their group of like-minded people. We need the perspective of others in our lives because it keeps us balanced. For any lifestyle choices that exist, you can find people who approve of your choice. If you surround yourself only with people who agree with you, you've created a bubble of yes men. The problem with that is you're not always right. None of us are. The Bible talks about renewing the mind and repenting (see Rom. 12:2).

*From that time Jesus began to preach and say, "Repent,
for the kingdom of heaven is at hand"* (Matthew 4:17
NASB).

In this verse here, Matthew 4:17, it says that Jesus cautioned,
"Repent, for the kingdom of heaven is at hand" (NASB). The word
repent is what we read in English when we read the Bible, but Jesus
didn't speak English. Sometimes the meaning of words can be lost in
translation because we don't see the depth of a word once it's translated, and sometimes words seem to lose their meaning to us because
many people have misused the word over a long stretch of time.
For a really long time I thought this word *repent* meant "to cry very
loud and feel sorry that you did a bad thing." That is not what this
means. If you look to see what the root word is in the Greek that is
translated to the word *repent*, you'll find the word *metanoeó*, which is
defined as "to change one's mind or purpose."[7] Every time I discover
a new truth that Christ has for me, I repent because I change my
mind about something. The time I realized and believed that God
wanted me to be prosperous, including receiving a financial blessing,
in order to be able to finance Kingdom exploits and to be a blessing
to others, I repented. I repented because up until then I had believed
that being poor was just a cross that Christians had to bear. I had
believed a lie, but then I discovered a new truth. I could have chosen
to justify the lie I had always believed, but instead, I kicked that lie
out and replaced it with the truth. I repented. Repenting is easy, and
it doesn't necessarily require that I lament and roll around in ashes
and sackcloth.

I crave diversity and absolutely enjoy hearing people who have a
completely different background than me explain things. They have
a perspective I've never experienced. They look at life through a different set of eyes. Their culture and their background are a type of

lens through which they view life. Their lens is different than mine, and I find that interesting. When people forget that they are viewing life through their own lens, they can get in the habit of thinking that their way is the only right way. I do believe that Jesus is the way, the truth, and the life; none come to the Father except through Jesus (see John 14:6). But a Christian life is going to look very different when walked out in different parts of the world and in different cultures. If you've ever met a group of people who believe that anything outside of their tiny little world is wrong, then you might be nodding your head in understanding at this point. There are actually people who believe that it's a sin to read anything other than the King James Version of the Bible. I was one of those people, and then one day a little lightbulb went off in my head when I realized that Jesus didn't speak English when He walked the earth as a man, so the KJV wasn't "the original" after all, despite what I've heard some say. There are actually people who are so absorbed in their small world and so immersed in their own culture that they truly believe that "different than them" equals evil or ungodly. I once spoke with someone who likened southern gospel hymns to a salad and contemporary praise and worship to candy. In other words, southern gospel hymns are what believers should mostly partake of because they feed our spirits like a salad feeds our bodies, but too much contemporary praise and worship is like eating too much candy. WHAT? I honestly wasn't sure what to say here so I asked, "What about believers living in Africa? How are they supposed to partake of these 'healthy salads'?" That's an absurd comparison to make. Jesus had a conversation in John 4:23: *"But the hour is coming, and is now here, when the true worshipers will worship the Father in spirit and truth..."* (ESV). What really matters is not what genre of music with which we worship God. What matters is that our worship comes from a place of sincerity in our hearts. Just like the posture of your worship doesn't matter. Some like to dance, some prefer to sit in their seats, while others lie down on the ground and worship God by soaking in His presence.

It's important that we see the Church as something global and not just what we can see. We're all unique individuals who were created to work together. I have something you need, and you have something I need. There are many visions, callings, and destinies in the same Body of Christ. All of us play a very important role in advancing the Kingdom of God. We all have a part to play. I'm no more important than you, and the guy on God TV is no more important or valuable than the camera guy who makes sure the camera is focused and pointed in the right direction from the right angle.

What we're doing here on earth is bigger than just you and me. This is about advancing the Kingdom of Heaven and releasing God's glory. I want you to love who you are because you are a carrier of His glory. You are an integral part of what God is doing in the earth today. There is a move of God that only you can fulfill. Many people are too busy wishing they were someone else to actually be who God has created them to be. They are cheating the whole world because they don't realize that when they are authentic, they are able to reach the people whom God has called them to reach. If you're a phenomenal soccer player but you spend your whole life trying to force yourself to forget all about soccer and be a violin player, how much sense does that make? The world needs what you bring to the table. You bring one thing to the table, and another person brings something different. Together we have this beautiful and diverse potluck dinner of gifts and talents that God will use to create a glorious movement in the earth. That's amazing.

CONFIDENCE

Confidence is about knowing who you are in Christ and knowing God has your back. When you begin to love who God created you to be, you'll know confidence. One huge key to having confidence is realizing we don't move in our own strength; we move in the strength of God.

> *Finally, be strong in the Lord and in His mighty power* (Ephesians 6:10).

There are probably at least three worship songs or Christian songs that I can think of right off the top of my head that capitalize on how weak we Christians are. For the life of me I do not understand why. We aren't weak because we are in Christ. I once was discussing this with a friend, and his reply was that *without Christ* we are weak. But I'm not without Him, and thankfully, I don't ever have to be. There are definitely times in our life when we may feel weak, but those are the times, more than ever, that we need to fortify and strengthen ourselves with the confidence that God IS with us. We don't have to minister out of our own supply of strength and power. We are in Christ, and His supply is ours now. He's given it to us.

> *For the Spirit God gave us does not make us timid, but gives us power, love and self-discipline* (2 Timothy 1:7).

> *Then the eleven disciples went to Galilee, to the mountain where Jesus had told them to go. When they saw Him, they worshiped Him; but some doubted. Then Jesus came to them and said, "All authority in heaven and on earth has been given to Me. Therefore go and make disciples of all nations, baptizing them in the name*

of the Father and of the Son and of the Holy Spirit, and
teaching them to obey everything I have commanded you.
And surely I am with you always, to the very end of the
age" (Matthew 28:16-20).

The end of the age of Moses to which Jesus referred here in verse 20 of Matthew 28 was no easy time to be alive. The Christians suffered great persecution at the hands of the apostate Jews and the religious community. Stephen was stoned to death, and Paul was imprisoned. If anyone needed to be reminded that Jesus would be with them, they really did. They were about to face things that were so grave that Jesus needed them to have the confidence of knowing that He had been given all authority in heaven and on earth and that He was commissioning them, yet they would not be alone. Jesus didn't tell them "until the very end of the age" because He no longer planned to be with believers after that point. He told them that because of the persecution they were about to experience. He knew it was going to be very important for them to really understand that during that time, although it might feel like God is far away, they wouldn't really be alone because He would be right there with them. This applies to you and me also. We are not alone when we are in a relationship with Jesus.

> *My prayer is not for them alone. I pray also for those*
> *who will believe in Me through their message, that all*
> *of them may be one, Father, just as You are in Me and*
> *I am in You. May they also be in Us so that the world*
> *may believe that You have sent Me. I have given them*
> *the glory that You gave Me, that they may be one as We*
> *are one—I in them and You in Me—so that they may*
> *be brought to complete unity* (John 17:20-23).

So Jesus is trying to drill the point home of the closeness and togetherness that we can and should experience with Him. He's praying out loud here. He is praying for the disciples, and He's praying for unity for the believers of that time. But He emphasizes His oneness with the Father and our oneness with Him. You are with Jesus, and Jesus is with you. You may have heard the song, "Jesus Loves Me," where it says that "they are weak but He is strong". I believe Jesus would like to step in here and say, "You are strong because I am strong."

> *Concerning this I implored the Lord three times that it might leave me. And He has said to me, "My grace is sufficient for you, **for power is perfected in weakness**." Most gladly, therefore, I will rather boast about my weaknesses, so that the power of Christ may dwell in me. Therefore I am well content with weaknesses, with insults, with distresses, with persecutions, with difficulties, for Christ's sake; for when I am weak, **then I am strong** (2 Corinthians 12:8-10 NASB).*

Read that very last line again that I bolded: *"…for when I am weak, then I am strong."*

You are not a mere human. You have every reason to be confident in who you are. You know you were intricately designed by God for something very special. It doesn't matter if you know what your big assignment here on earth is right now. Your number-one calling is to love God and be loved by Him. You can park the car right there and just get really good at receiving His love. The reason I feel very free to say that is not because I want you to sit around doing nothing but receiving His love. The reason I feel free to say something like that is because His love motivates and fuels everything I do. When you're in a posture to just soak up the love that He's already given, it's like fuel in your tank to go be His hands and feet to a world that doesn't yet know that it is loved by the God of heaven.

The word *confidence* appears so many times in Scripture. God wants you to have confidence, but the big question is, "In what?"

We have Christ. We are redeemed. We can place our confidence fully in Christ. He has our back. We can walk, rule, and reign with authority on the earth because the God of the universe is in our corner. When I decree a thing, I do it with confidence because I know it is power-packed. God's power lives inside of you as a believer. The same resurrection power that raised Christ from the dead is at your disposal. God is our source of power, our source of strength, and our reason for having confidence.

You can be confident in His design, His plans, and His goodness. You can be confident that He created you with excellence to be a being of excellence. I believe it's the Lord's will for us to walk in confidence through life. No matter what you may come up against in life, we have confidence knowing that we are not alone. Christ is with you. You are IN CHRIST, and you have the capability of resting in Him. You are protected in Him. You are powerful in Him. You are completed and made whole by Him. In Christ you lack no good thing and you have every spiritual gift, according to First Corinthians 1:7.

Because you are God's creation, you have value and worth. Your value, your worth, and your beauty do not come from having the best hair stylist, from wearing designer makeup, or from what size jeans you wear. You are beautiful because you are God's child. He created you, and it is He, not society or culture, who has called YOU lovely. Be confident in who He created you to be. The style you love, the interests and likes you have, the quirks and loud laugh that you have—those are all aspects of your personality that God created to make you YOU. You're you because of those aspects of your character created by the Father. When you stifle who you are, you stifle the flow of His glory through you. Shine, baby!

Chapter 5

PURITY, MODESTY, AND BIBLICAL SEXUALITY

PURITY

I believe that it's imperative that we as Christians shift our way of thinking about purity. Purity is a way of thinking and not necessarily a rule that says, "Don't have sex so that you remain pure." Remember that Jesus says in Matthew 5:28: *"But I say, anyone who even looks at a woman with lust has already committed adultery with her in his heart"* (NLT).

With His words in mind, I ask, isn't purity a posture of the heart rather than a rule that says, "Don't have sex until you're married"?

Purity is not the same thing as virginity.

The Church has dropped the ball when it comes to teaching about purity. If you grew up in church, you probably heard some of the analogies used to describe purity. Depending on your youth pastor, you may have heard you would be a dirty piece of chewed-up bubble gum if you decided to have sex before you were married.

You also may have heard that you would be like a crumpled-up piece of paper. I know there are more terribly awful analogies out there that have made other young ladies (and probably young men) feel like worthless people who have blown it big time. All these analogies make it sound as if purity is about what you do, rather than a mindset. Purity is a way of thinking; purity is not adhering to a list of rules and keeping your virginity. Trust me, you can keep your virginity intact and still compromise your values. There are plenty of sex acts out there that can make you feel really used.

These analogies are just not fitting. They are disrespectful, and I do not believe they offer an aspect of redemption. They condemn, whereas Jesus didn't come to condemn but rather to restore (see John 3:17; 12:47). If the analogy doesn't contain an aspect of restoration, which none of these do, then we have no business using it as a piece of manipulation to keep teens from having sex. As a matter of fact, we just don't have any right manipulating other people to do what we believe is right. Even if what we believe is right really is right, we do not have the right to attempt to control other people. What we can do is equip them and teach them to hear God speak to them. You cannot shame teenagers into doing the "right thing." Shame does the opposite.

If you are reading this and you have blown it, I have good news: Jesus makes us a new creation (see 2 Cor. 5:17). He restores us one hundred percent. Later on you will hear my testimony, including the poor choices I made in relationships. But even despite my promiscuity and having done other things of which I was ashamed, on the day of my marriage, I was every bit as PURE as the Duggar girl who saved her first kiss for her wedding day, and privately at that! There was no difference in my purity and hers! Even after all I had done. My purity was completely intact. I wasn't unclean, and neither are you!

MODESTY

Something has really bugged me for many years, but I've only recently been able to put into words how I felt about this topic of modesty. I believe that the idea of modesty has been very misunderstood. It's almost like someone somewhere drew up this list of rules, sort of like a dress code, and decided that this would define what's "modest," but there is no such list in Scripture anywhere. One of the main problems with creating rules for modesty is that someone else can always come along and decide to draw up a stricter set of rules because that person wants to be "even more modest."

Modesty is not a dress code. Modesty is not about covering nakedness. Modesty is a posture of the heart.

Venture with me so I can explain.

One woman has decided that modesty is a long skirt and not a pair of jeans because those curve around the legs and buttocks. She believes that this skirt "is more modest." She wears sleeves that cover her arms, at least down to her elbows. She believes in her heart that this is pleasing to God. Maybe she didn't decide this on her own. Maybe that's what her mother believed. Maybe that's what her mother's mother believed. To this woman, it is modest to wear no makeup and no jewelry. She believes she is being modest by avoiding these "worldly" things. In her heart, she is doing this because she loves God. This is all she's ever known, and she believes deep down in her heart that she is dressing by these rules or standards because she loves God.

On the other side of the world, a young woman in a tribe in the Congo of Africa hears about the Savior Jesus who died so that she could be a friend to God. She believes with her whole heart and begins walking and talking with Jesus daily. She begins raising her children up to know and love God as well. She prays with them, and together they sing praises to Him. This woman loves God. Like all the other women she's ever known in her tribe, she walks around topless. It's hot where she lives, and every woman she's ever known walks around with her breasts exposed. In her culture women do not wear tops. They wear bottoms. It has never crossed her mind that this would be immodest to anyone else, especially the other girl on the other side of the world in an air-conditioned building with a skirt down to her feet and sleeves to her elbow, because this is all she has ever known. She knows deep down in her heart that she loves God and that she walks with Him. She is modest.

Who is right?

When I first got saved, I was the woman described in the first paragraph because I did what I believed I was supposed to do. "People that love God dress a certain way," I thought. That's what modesty is: dressing a certain way. Well, that's what I thought at that time, at least. It's hard to remember that far back, but something about this must not have sat well in my heart because I began to search for more answers. Some of my questions were, "Why do we dress this way? Who said God wanted this?"

I knew I loved God, and I knew I would obey Him till the end of my life. I was completely ready to live a life of complete "separation" when it came to my clothing. So I began to seek Him. I began to dig into Scripture, I began to ask the Holy Spirit questions, and I began to ask people questions. The digging into Scripture part and the asking the Holy Spirit part went over a lot smoother than the "asking people" part. When people have a deep-rooted belief in something, especially when this is a belief that has been passed down from generation to generation, it becomes very important to them. If you come along and try to question this belief, it is very unsettling to them, and many times it can be very hard for them to receive what is being said because it's just too hard to embrace the thought that they might have been wrong all these years. It's not about being wrong though.

One of the questions I began searching out in the Word, asking the Holy Spirit about, and asking people about was, "Why do we dress this way?" The main Scripture I was given to explain why we wore dresses was the following verse:

> *A woman shall not wear man's clothing, nor shall a man put on a woman's clothing; for whoever does these things is an abomination to the Lord your God* (Deuteronomy 22:5 NASB).

This raised many more questions for me, as I did not understand how people came to interpret that verse to mean that women should wear long skirts. As a very new Christian, my thought was that God was giving this law because if a woman were to present herself as a man, or vice versa, that it would be deceptive. If a man or a woman is attempting to trick someone else by disguising himself or herself as a member of the opposite sex, to me, a very new Christian, it could cause deception, hurt, confusion, and so it sounded logical that God would make this law for Israel. Also, what made us come to the conclusion that God was designating dresses for women? When did God ever say, "Dresses are for women. Pants are for the bros"? He didn't. I mean, I sure can't find it in Scripture, at least. In fact, during the time that this was written, men and women both wore robes.

Furthermore, in Deuteronomy, we also have laws about not trimming your beard and not wearing clothing with linen and wool woven together. If someone is going to try to yoke someone with one Old Covenant law, I have to ask in return if he trims his beard or wears linen and wool together. Remember the chapter in the beginning of this book called "Laying a Foundation: Understanding the New and Better Covenant"? Well, if you skipped it or don't remember it, this would be a great time to glance back so it will make sense to you why the Old Covenant Law can't be picked apart and applied to New Covenant Christians. In the New Covenant, we are led by Love Himself. Modesty isn't a dress code invented by man.

The truth of the matter is this: regardless of our sex, if our motivation in our fashion/clothing choices is to entice and arouse other people sexually, then we just aren't walking in love. This is going to look different in each believer's life. Think back to the example I used at the beginning of this chapter about the two different women. They both had very different opinions about what constitutes modesty. Modesty looks way different in the lives of believers across the world. Where we mess this thing up is when we decide what is modest for us and we begin to make rules about what defines modesty for other people. During the time that Scripture was written, people had certain ideas and thoughts about what modesty was to their culture. I feel quite certain that those thoughts and ideas are very different than the ones held by people alive today. One thing is certain: we don't have the right to determine what is modest for other people. We don't have the right to create rules by which we expect others to live. If we will promote loving God and loving others as our highest priority, the rest will fall into place. Yes, there will be tough questions and unexpected scenarios in which believers will find themselves, but with the love of God as the fuel in our tank, we can make the choice to honor others. Freedom can feel scary to some people, which is why the natural human inclination can be to create rules and laws for other people to follow, but freedom is worth it. When freedom and the love of God and others go together, we can be assured that the outcome is going to be good.

I know that many people are of the opinion that "dressing modestly" alludes to the notion that it is a woman's job to make sure she doesn't cause men to lust after her. I want to be really clear here about something: it is not YOUR job to make sure SOMEONE ELSE doesn't sin. You can't do that, anyways. If a person lets sin reign in his heart, then you could take him to a deserted island and drop him off with no human contact and no external influence and he would still sin because he's allowed sin to be his master. This is just the case with some people. You were not created to have control over another person. You were created to have control over yourself. It is called self-control, and it is one of the fruits of the Spirit mentioned in Galatians (see Gal. 5:23). You are in charge of making sure YOU don't sin. Nobody else. You are not an animal, driven by instinct. Men are not animals, and it is about time we as women and mothers stop raising up our boys believing the lie that they don't have the power to take their thoughts captive and submit them to the obedience of Christ Jesus (see 2 Cor. 10:5). We cannot take the responsibility upon ourselves that we have the power to stop other people from sinning. Even if a woman is dressed in a way where she is covered from head to toe, there will always be someone somewhere with, say, a wrist fetish, and so on. Modesty is a posture of the heart, between a person and God. It's really important to realize here that God did create the human body and He did originally create humans naked. Gasp! Yes, naked. Could it be that it is actually humans who have objectified one another to the point where women and men alike have become obsessed with sexualizing the human body? Don't worry. I'm not trying to convince you to join a nudist colony, but we've been redeemed from the curse. Jesus broke every curse for those who would abide in Him, and in the beginning when we were originally created, Genesis says that Adam and

Eve were naked and they were unashamed (see Gen. 2:25). Could it be that the human body wasn't intended to be sexualized and objectified in the way that our society does? I think so. Keep in mind that I'm really and truly not trying to talk you into becoming a nudist. I like clothes. I want you to wear clothes too, but it's important to realize that we are redeemed from every curse because of Jesus and that affects this topic of modesty as well. Was naked Eve modest?

Now that I may or may not have offended all of you by going on about nakedness, I will say that I'm not trying to offend you; I'm simply trying to get you to think about this outside the box, in a different way than you may have been raised to think. I want you to think about this from a new perspective. We as believers should not TRY to offend others outright. With that being said, let me go on to say this (you know me. I'm all about balance, so allow me to balance this out a little): no matter how careful of a life you live, somebody somewhere will be offended at your choices. I'm in no way suggesting that you should walk around on eggshells, hiding who you are so that others are not offended by the way you live a life of freedom. If I go to a place that has certain customs and traditions, I honor those people by respecting their way of life. For example, certain cultures take their shoes off at the door, and they would feel very offended and disrespected if you were to come in their home without taking off your shoes. Even if you're not superstitious and you know that what really matters is in the heart, by offending them on purpose, you're closing them off from hearing the message of love that you carry. Is that really what you want? Of course it's not. We can't live our lives by other people's convictions, standards, rules, and traditions. We need to each be led by the Holy Spirit and walk in the love of God.

SEXUALITY AND LOVE

Repeat after me: *Sex is not bad. Sex is not evil.* God invented sex, and He knew ahead of time that we would enjoy it. God created us as beings capable of sexuality. Our bodies are specifically designed to find pleasure in sex. Do you think that was a mistake? I fully believe, after having read the whole Bible, that God created sex to be between a woman and her husband. Anything outside of that will lead to hurt and heartache, and that's just not God's best for our lives. I've lived that story too many times over.

One of the reasons why the Book of Solomon, I believe, is in the Bible, is because God wanted us to see this raw, healthy sexuality between a man and his wife. I don't know where anyone ever got the idea that Christians had to be prudes. I know there are a lot of stereotypes out there about women, but as a woman, I really love sex. I enjoy having sex with my husband and can only think of a handful of times that my husband ever wanted to have sex that I didn't also want to have sex. I want to say something without anyone getting really offended with me: if you're married and you're not **enjoying** sex with your husband, there's likely a deeper issue. I'm not saying you're broken or that there's something wrong with you. I know that there are definitely health issues that exist that also sometimes keep people from fully enjoying intercourse. I, of course, want all people to walk in health, and I believe God wants that for them as well. This is not a book about healing, but in those cases, I would hope you would pursue healing. There is a natural aspect to healing, because I believe God has given naturopaths, holistic doctors, and medical doctors the wisdom to help people get to the bottom of physical ailments. There is also a spiritual side of healing where we pray for healing, ask others to pray for us, get anointed with oil, etc. If you are reading this and you don't enjoy sex with your husband or wife for health reasons, I pray that even as you read these words, you would be supernaturally healed. I believe there is power in this chapter because by faith I am writing what God has ministered to me personally. If you're not already healed—because I truly do feel the anointing on this as I write it—I have included an activation prayer at the end of this chapter.

Aside from physical ailments, there are times when people aren't able to enjoy intimacy with their spouse because of wounds of the heart. These can be harder to sort through because they aren't always treated with the same credibility as a health problem. With a health issue, at least, a doctor can tell you, "This is what's wrong," but with wounds of the heart, no doctor will be able to pinpoint the problem, unless maybe your doctor is prophetic. That would be pretty cool, actually, if my doctor got a word of knowledge or prophecy for me. Hey, make me an appointment with that doctor, please! In all seriousness, I want to tell you that I believe God wants you healed and whole even more than you want to be healed and whole. Jesus didn't just die on the cross to make a way for you to go to heaven. No, your salvation entails much more than just a "get-to-heaven-free card." When you were born again, you became an ambassador of heaven, and because of that, now you are responsible for bringing heaven to earth. But that's not all! I feel like I'm the host of *The Price is Right*, telling folks what they've won. Salvation is much more amazing than many of us have been taught in church.

Acts 2:21 says: *"And everyone who calls on the name of the Lord will be **saved**."*

This is just amazing, so pay close attention to what I'm saying here. See that word that I bolded at the end of the sentence? *Saved.* We all have an idea of what that word means TO US, but what is this word supposed to mean to us? I don't feel that the English language captures its true connotation. The root word there is the word *sózó*. When we look that word up in the *Strong's Exhaustive Concordance*, we can find the meaning of the root word, the original word that was in the earliest manuscripts, which we have translated into the English word *saved*. Let's take a look:

> heal, be made whole.
>
> From a primary sos (contraction for obsolete saos, "safe");
> to save, i.e., Deliver or protect (literally or figuratively)—
> heal, preserve, save (self), do well, be (make) whole.[8]

That, my friends, is what Jesus did for you when He "saved" you. That is no piddly little "get-to-heaven-free card." That, my friends, is what we call down in Texas "the WHOLE enchilada." He healed you, made you whole, saved you, protects you, preserves you, and makes you well. Sometimes we don't experience all aspects of our salvation because we didn't know it was available. Think about it this way: How are you saved? By faith through grace (see Eph. 2:8). So if I'm saved (*sózó*) by faith, then I am able to access all parts of my salvation (*sózó*) by faith as well. All the gifts God has for you are available to you by faith. **Faith is not so much believing God will come through as it is refusing even to entertain the notion that He might not.** It's hard to have faith for something that you didn't even know was possible. That's why I believe that many people will read this chapter and experience healing—because now they know that not only is it possible, it is rightfully theirs.

I already can hear that Marvin Gaye song, "Sexual Healing," playing in the background. Maybe that's what I should have named this chapter, but I figured some of y'all don't know about that world. I'm just being silly here so you'll remember what I'm saying, but there's something prophetic about it. God truly desires to bring some sexual healing to you and to your marriage.

There are different types of love. The love between a woman and her husband is different than the love they have for their children. It just is. In the English language, there's not a lot of versatility with the word *love*. I *love* my mom. I *love* ice cream. It's the same word, but there's a very different meaning behind it when I use it in various ways. Sadly, it's just thrown around. I know this teenage boy, and he currently has a girlfriend. He usually has a girlfriend, just never the same one. He's a handsome young guy, about sixteen years old now, I think. It seems that within a week of "going out" together, he and his girlfriend are confessing their undying love to one another. We also happen to be friends on Facebook so I get to see the girls roll by so quickly that one girl will be in his profile pics with him when he meets the next one. He apparently gave his password to the most recent girl because she logged in as him, and from his Facebook page, she posted a love ballad to rival all love ballads. According to her, she came alive four days ago when she met him, and she knows they are soul mates, and when his lips touch hers, she knows her reason for being alive. I really wish I could tell you I'm kidding. This is not love. This is caused by raging hormones and little to no self-control and could be compounded by the fact that nobody in the girl's life ever taught her ahead of time about real love. Some of this is caused by the hunger that every person has to be known and loved fully by another.

Let's talk about the word *love* again. As I said before, in the English language, we only have the one word, and then beyond that we have to use other words to describe what we mean. In the Greek language, in which much of our Scriptures are originally written, there is more than just the one word for *love*. I actually found six, but only five of them are used in Scripture. I'm just going to talk about three because I find them relevant to what we are discussing. The three words are *agape*, *phileo*, and *eros*.

1. **Agape** is unconditional love, like the love of the Father. This is an accurate way to describe the way God loves us unconditionally and also the way that we, as God's children, are able to love. In fact, John 15:12 uses that root word of *agape* to describe how God is asking us to love others:

> *My command is this: Love each other as I have loved you* (John 15:12).

It's because He loves us and He is our source of love that we can love others. In fact, when we receive God's love, we are able to have a river of His love flowing out of us. Because of that, we are able to love the people that society has deemed unlovable.

2. **Phileo** is the type of love experienced in a friendship. The city Philadelphia is named after this type of love and is known as the "city of brotherly love." *Phileo* is a committed type of love, one that you choose.

3. **Eros** is a love with sexual passion. This word implies intimacy and sexual desire. The word *erotic* comes from this word *eros*. This is the love of lovers.

Now the reason I even went there with these types of love is because I have found that a good marriage requires that we love our spouse with all three of these. I may not always look at my husband and want to rip his clothes off (I have to be honest, most of the time I totally do), but I can always love him with choice and determination. *Agape* love helps me decide to love people in advance, even when I know they may not love me in return. That helps keep a marriage relationship alive because it implies that we've decided ahead of time to love and forgive. *Phileo* love is important to a marriage relationship because it allows us to be there for each other in those times when we need a friend in whom we can confide. Of course our spouse isn't our only friend, but he or she is there for us. It's important that the *phileo* love of friendship be there so that you enjoy one another and have fun together. Last but not least, *eros* love is important because it's the love that keeps our sex life alive. Without any one of these three, we're not really enjoying our spouse fully.

I want to pray for you right now, and I speak this prayer over you with faith in the healing power of God. I also believe in the power of written and spoken words declared in faith. I ask that if you are able, read this out loud, and declare it with authority.

ACTIVATION

With the authority given to me in Christ Jesus, I declare your sex drive healed, whole, and normal. I realize that will look different in each person and each married couple. I declare your hormones and reproductive system healed and whole. I speak healing over your emotions, your memories, and your past. I speak to your spirit and declare you are a new creation and your conscience is cleansed from the shame of the past. Let go of any condemnation because there is no condemnation in Christ. You are not defined by what has happened to you. If someone stole your virginity, I declare to you that they did not steal your purity. Your purity was given to you anew in Christ Jesus, and He restores even your virginity. You are loved and healed by the Father's embrace. Just rest in His arms right now. Wherever you're at, I want you to take a moment to meditate on His raw love for you. Breathe in His love. Exhale any shame and condemnation that is left. Do that again. Breathe in His love...exhale and release shame and condemnation. Say aloud, "I reject shame and condemnation. I forgive myself. I love myself because God loves me."

~~~

Chapter 6

DATING VS. COURTING

Before you hear me talk about dating, courting, or anything involving relationships, I think it's only fair that you hear a part of my story that isn't so pretty. I'm not ashamed of my past, and I believe I am redeemed and am a new creation. I almost feel as though I'm about to tell you someone else's story. Ultimately, I believe God has taken what was meant to destroy me and disqualify me and He's instead worked it together for good. That's what He does (see Rom. 8:28). It's pretty amazing. Take a stroll with me down my own memory lane. Some of this might be hard to hear, but it's my journey; and God turned my mess into a message.

Before I entered into a close relationship with God, I spent my teenage and young adult years craving love from people, especially guys. I've always had a loving and close relationship with my dad, so it wasn't like I had daddy issues, but I desperately wanted someone to love me. I had this yearning inside of me to be loved and adored deeply by someone else. I can think of several very unhealthy relationships that I had before the age of twenty-one, one of which was when I was sixteen years old. I remember I met this particular guy named James, by whom I was intrigued, at a restaurant/bar/grill type of place, where people often came to play pool. James was playing pool, and I met him on a Thursday night at this local hot spot. One thing that made this relationship so unhealthy is that James was twenty-three years old. I was in a very unhealthy relationship with James for almost two years, and I hid it from my parents. He would cheat on me around town. One of my closest friends from school had told me that she thought I needed to stop seeing him before he hurt me, but whatever she could see, I was blind to it. People would tell me that he was unfaithful to me, but the day I found out for myself, it broke my heart and made me feel like nothing. I drove by his house one day when he said he wouldn't be home, and not only was he there, but an ex-girlfriend's car was there. My heart was broken, and I knew that he didn't really love me. It was that day that I realized he was using me. I felt like a fool. The next day I went to his aunt's house to let him know that I knew he had cheated on me and to break up with him. I remember looking at the unmoved expression on his face and thinking, "He does not care that I'm hurting. He truly feels nothing. He has been using me. I am a naive idiot." I left his aunt's house and got in my car. My hand was shaking as I reached for the car door and got out my keys. I slowly put the keys in the ignition of my little red Honda Civic del Sol, and I remember praying to God that he would come running out that front door to ask me not to leave. I imagined him rushing out the door with tears in his eyes, but the door stayed closed. I prayed to God, "Please let him come after me" as I slowly put my car in drive. He didn't, though. I pulled away feeling so worthless and stupid. How could I have been so desperate, and how could I have given my heart to someone who didn't even love me in return?

The truth was that I was a beautiful girl who just didn't know her worth. Even in the midst of all the bad decisions, sin, and mistakes, I was so valuable to God; I just didn't know it. And the feeling of emptiness I had came from not knowing God and also from not knowing how much God loved me. I had an insatiable hunger for love, and Jesus was more than ready to fill that yearning in my heart, but instead I was searching for validation from men—and at one point even women—who, in return, treated me as a sexual object. At this point, I wish I could tell you that I turned to Jesus and we lived happily ever after, but instead my life kind of spiraled out of control for the next five years. My life gradually became a much darker place, and the decisions I made dug deeper and deeper into a lifestyle that contradicted my own standards and morals. I ended up with many other guys who also were all basically using me. I could tell you at least five more heartbreaking stories from other unhealthy relationships in which I managed to find myself. Again and again I found myself looking for my worth in the acceptance of others, specifically men. This yearning that I felt inside of me led me from one dangerous situation to another, and I always felt like something was missing from me.

Thankfully and obviously, my story didn't end there. God had a really cool plan to help me understand that He wanted to fill that aching void inside of me. Toward the end of my high school years, I started smoking cigarettes, smoking weed, and binge drinking at parties. I have always been a social butterfly and the life of the party. I've always been an extrovert. I love people so I had many friends, and my senior year I was voted both "class clown" and "most daring." That's a dangerous combination right there. If you had asked me at the time, I would have told you that I loved everyone in my school and everyone loved me. I went to a small country high school so I can say with great certainty that everyone knew about me. I was known for being a party girl with the vocabulary of a seasoned sailor, always happy to make everyone laugh.

When I graduated from high school, I did what was expected of me: I went to college. I also really believed at the time that it was what I wanted as well. I was accepted at UT Tyler, and I moved about an hour and a half from my hometown to a land far, far away to try a new venture unlike anything I had ever done before. I was in for a very rude awakening. College was nothing like high school, where everyone knew my name. I was a nobody on that huge college campus, and that feeling of lostness ate at my soul in a way like I had never before experienced. I walked the sidewalks between classes trying to make eye contact, hoping to find a friend in someone, but time passed without me being able to make any connections. I had a part-time job at the time, and I had met a few people, one of whom I'm still friends with, but the shock of how different life had become was just too much to bear. One of the major differences was that there was no support system there to catch me as I was falling and spiraling out of control. No momma, no daddy, no friends, no high school entourage of friends...nothing. I felt so alone, and on top of that, I was shocked to realize that I wasn't going to be able to make it through college the same way I had made it through high school. In high school, I rarely had to study, yet I still managed to pass my classes and do well most of the time. But in college, not only was I not doing well at keeping up my grades, I chronically skipped classes until I just stopped showing up. No one was there to tell me what to do. Time marched on until I flunked out of school, and because of the stress, pressure, and shame that I felt, I began to take prescription tranquilizer pills, anxiety medicine, and pain pills just to try to numb the painful feelings I felt inside me. I felt like such a failure, and I didn't want to have to see the disappointed looks on the faces of my family members as they found out that I didn't make it. I failed, and I felt like a failure in every sense of the word.

Around this time, I overdosed on alcohol and anxiety meds. I ended up having my stomach pumped at the local hospital. My dad found out that I had stopped going to my classes, and he came to Tyler, packed me up, and moved me back to Paris. I enrolled in the junior college there, and although I did fairly well in school and connected with old friends, I met some new friends and found new drugs. I began to experiment with cocaine, meth, and ecstasy. At one point, at my rock bottom, I went on a week-ong meth binge, and during the times when I was high, I did things that made me feel ashamed of myself. Once I came down, the effects of the drug were gone, but the memories of the things I had done were still there, chiseled into my memory, which caused me to struggle with feelings of hopelessness and shame more intensely than ever before. At my all-time low, directly after that weeklong binge, I found out that I was pregnant. As if it wasn't already really bad news that I was pregnant, on top of that, I wasn't even completely sure who had fathered the child. That's not a fun situation to be in. I felt so ashamed of myself and of my choices. I talked individually with the two men who might have fathered the child, and the very short version of the story is that one basically began to try to dominate, control, and abuse me, while the other wanted nothing to do with me and ever so vaguely insinuated to me that it might be in everyone's best interest for me have an abortion. I also wanted an abortion. I had already been thinking about it, and although he didn't come out and bluntly say it, I felt that's what he was alluding to.

I want to pause here for a second so I can interject something I am very passionate about. A lot of Christians seem to talk about women who have had abortions like they are evil, murdering monsters who deserve to burn in hell. God is not angry and disgusted with people who are lost in sin, making terrible decisions, and being tormented by thoughts from the enemy. He is merciful and forgiving. His hands are reaching out to those in need, so just maybe, as Christians, our hands should also be reaching out rather than doubled into angry shaking fists. At one point, surely, you've seen the angry protestors outside an abortion clinic, or maybe at least you've seen an angry anti-abortion bumper sticker somewhere. The flaw with that way of thinking is that many (if not most) women and young ladies who do choose abortion hate themselves twice as much as the angry people marching with the picket signs and clenched fists do. We're not reaching these women with our anger. We are driving them into the arms of the enemy by being rude and disrespectful to them.

I believe that at this point in my life, my all-time low, that satan sent numerous specific demons to go and terrorize me with these thoughts:

"No baby deserves to be born to you."

"You can't even take care of yourself. How are you gonna take care of a baby?"

"You've done drugs. What if your baby is mentally retarded or has deformities because of you?"

"Your baby will be in heaven with God. You would be doing this baby a favor by aborting it."

I was a tormented soul. I hated myself for all the things I had done, and I truly felt like the scum of the earth. I was disgusted at my own choices. I didn't believe any child deserved to be born to me. I knew that before babies are born, they are in heaven with God, and I thought that if I had an abortion, my baby would just be with God again. To me that sounded like a much better option than having to be born to someone like me and to have to grow up with me as a mother. I began to ask around to find out where I could go to get an abortion.

One person gave me an address and said, "Go here. They can help you get an abortion."

I called that day and made myself an appointment. It was a place called the Paris Pregnancy Care Center. The place is still there, still run by the same beautiful woman, Vicki Powell. I highly encourage you to look them up and sow into what she is doing there, if you can. When I got there, the first thing I did was take a pregnancy test. I was like four months along so it was, of course, positive. When the lady came and talked to me, she eventually brought up Jesus, and she told me how much He loved me. I felt so shocked and angry. That's not what I came there for! I remember yelling at her, "I know who Jesus is! And if you knew Him, you would know that He doesn't even like me right now!" I stormed out of the office that day, and I didn't know it at the time, but today I nearly know that little lady hit her knees and began praying for God to intervene in my life. All paths started leading toward Him at this point. I couldn't seem to come up with the money to get an abortion. It was not a lot of money, and yet I could not, for the life of me, come up with it. One sad and lonely night, I came to the conclusion that I was stuck with no way out of becoming a mother. I decided to do my best to continue my pregnancy with no more drugs, and I was going to attempt to be a good person. I spent the duration of my pregnancy trying to just get my crap together. At one point, I remembered something that lady at the Paris Pregnancy Care Center had mentioned to me. She had mentioned some parenting videos that day, and so I decided to go back and ask to watch them. She told me they had a system where girls could come in and watch these videos in exchange for "mommy dollars." Mommy dollars were little dollars that were cut out of copy paper. They could be spent in a special room of the center called "the boutique." In the boutique there were diapers, baby clothes, and sometimes car seats and baby swings. You could buy the things in the boutique with mommy dollars. Honestly, it is a really brilliant system! Eventually I had gone through all the videos that the center had, and one of the counselors told me that there was a Bible study on Tuesday nights, if I wanted to come, and they served dinner. She told me that you get three mommy dollars for going to Bible study, so I decided to go.

I didn't know it at the time, but that was a divine setup. I went and met a woman named Michelle along with so many other amazing women who are still in my life today. Michelle had something I like to call "gloves-off love." Let me explain. If you accidentally threw something away in a big dirty dumpster, like, let's say, your cell phone, you would probably want to wear some gloves to go through that thing. Well, my life felt to me at the time like that big dirty dumpster, and that's kind of how I was used to being treated by Christians who thought they were better than someone with a reputation like mine. Michelle didn't care. I had told her so much of the horrible things I had done, and yet she loved me with that sweet, Christlike, gloves-off love. I will never forget how special she made me feel and how kind she was to each girl who came to Bible study. The months marched on, and Tuesday after Tuesday, I heard Michelle talk about the love of God and how He loves everyone. She talked about how salvation is a free gift, one that you receive by faith. That was a very different idea than that which I had in my head about what salvation was. I had the idea that salvation was something that involved abiding by a list of rules created by Jesus—that I needed to follow these, go to church, get my life cleaned up, and then Jesus would love me and I'd be saved.

I still remember going to church sporadically when I was in my early teenage years, and I remember a couple of occasions when I was at church, an altar call was given for people to "get right with Jesus." One time I decided to go down. I felt like a scumbag because of all the bad things I had done, and so I had myself a good, long cry, and I got up feeling really good. I remember this one particular day after this had happened. I was driving home in my little car. It was a bright and sunny day, and I had felt refreshed, hopeful, and really clean as I drove home. I remember looking into the clouds thinking, "Wow. I feel so good right now. If only Jesus would return now before I screw up again...." I just didn't quite understand salvation back then. I had always thought of salvation as some slippery and fleeting thing—hard to get and hard to keep.

But these Bible study classes were opening up my eyes to a side of God that I didn't even realize was there. I started to entertain the notion that God may not have been who I thought He was all these years.

On January 15, 2006, I gave birth to my son, Joseph Emanuel... the child that almost wasn't. Oh my dear, sweet God, thank You for intervening in my life. Every year that we celebrate Joseph's birthday, I look at that boy and sob with joy and gratitude for who he is and that God intervened in my life. From the depths of my soul, thankfulness and joy spill out when I think of how good God has been to me. What a perfect miracle he was. With his fuzzy black hair and tiny round face, he was the most beautiful little thing on which I had ever laid eyes. I looked at this child and was swept away by so much emotion. Three days after he was born, I sat in my hospital room filling out Joseph's baby book. I was writing all the information in when I came to the section about the father. It was then that the severity of my situation was staring me in the face.

"Here I am," I thought. "All alone, with no husband, not even so much as a boyfriend, and no father who will be happy to see my child and love him like I do." It was at that moment that I felt another Presence step into that hospital room. I do realize God is omnipresent and therefore present everywhere at once, but a tangible Presence stepped into my hospital room that day. I knew beyond a shadow of a doubt that God Himself was in that room. I was trembling as tears began to spill down my cheeks. I remember so clearly hearing Him say to me, "I love you." I felt those words echo through my being like a resounding gong. In that room, without even knowing at the time what it was, I had a vision where God took me back in my memory to the worst day of my life. On that particular day to which God brought me, I had done the most shameful acts ever. It was the memory of that weeklong meth binge, my all-time low. On this day that had haunted me for some time, I compromised the morals with which I had been raised. I said to God, "Why would You show me this?"

"I LOVED YOU THEN," He whispered.

That was all I needed to know. The floodgates of tears were open, and there, in the hospital room, not at a church altar, I had a supernatural encounter with the God of the universe, my Creator, and my new best friend. This shook me to my core. In the back of the baby book in which I had been writing, I turned to a blank page and I began to write two letters. The first letter I wrote was to God. I told Him I loved Him too and that I'd made a real mess of my life. "I have lied to the people who loved me the most," I said. "I have burned bridges and screwed over people who trusted me," I said.

"My life is in shambles, but if You loved me then, then I know You love me now. Please help me turn this mess around."

The second letter was to my sweet little Joseph. I wrote a letter telling him that I promised to love him, be the best mom I could be, and that I would do everything I could to raise him up to be a mighty man of God.

Now I told you all of that to set the stage for you, but not only that—I need you to know my story. I need you to know who I am and where I have come from. I do not write to you as a woman who has made all the right choices. I don't even write to you as a woman who has made only a few mistakes. I do not write to you as some preacher lady with a spotless past. I write to you as a woman who at one point wished she could just die because of the shame and embarrassment of her own past. God is faithful. I write to you as a woman who once smoked meth and snorted coke but who now stays high in the glory and joy of God. HA! It's a cheaper fix, and I never have to experience a comedown.

The good thing about grace is that it will meet you anywhere. The even better thing about grace is that it will not leave you there.

When I became a Christian, I realized that I wanted my dating experience to be different than it had been in the past. I just wanted to change the way I had approached dating because the way I went about it previously hadn't yielded good results. One thing I found was that there weren't really many people who could give me applicable dating tips to my unique life situation. I already had a baby. I lived alone, in my own apartment, with my little baby Joseph. I felt very eager for God to send me a husband. I really wanted to share my life with someone—someone to laugh with and someone to call my companion. I loved God and knew that I wasn't alone in life, but I did have this hope that God also had a man for me. I didn't really have any idea how God expected me to find a husband, nor did I know whether or not He even *had* any specific ways that dating was supposed to go in general. I felt surely He should have written some sort of a manual on something as complicated as finding a mate, but alas, my search for such a manual came up fruitless. At that point, I just knew I didn't want to date in the same way that I had *before* getting saved, because that had already proved to be a disaster.

A friend of mine set me up on a date with this guy. We'll call him Ben. Ben was what we term down in Texas "a good ol' boy." He had his own truck, wasn't depending on his parents anymore, had a good job, and stayed out of trouble. His background was Baptist, he loved God, and even though at the time I considered myself to be a Holiness Pentecostal, I thought that our differences in beliefs weren't so huge that there would be problems. Overall, he was a really great guy. We went on several dates, and I brought my baby boy along. Ben was very nice to my son, Joseph, and soon I realized that though I really liked Ben, I didn't feel any kind of romantic affection for him at all. I wasn't really sure what that meant for us, but I knew it wouldn't be fair to Ben or my son for me to keep this relationship going along without considering whether or not there would ever be a future in marriage between Ben and me. I began to pray about things. I thought it was possible that my lack of romantic feelings for Ben may have been a sign that there was someone different out there that God had for me. Now I hadn't been saved very long, but I had a great relationship with the Holy Spirit, and often I would hear Him talk to me about things. The problem was that things would get all cloudy for me whenever strong emotion was involved, which was clearly the case here. I didn't want to hurt Ben's feelings. I also didn't want to make a mistake and end up wishing I hadn't sent a good guy away. I desired a husband, and here was this great guy, Ben, who seemed to have it all together. But, on the other hand, I was pretty sure that I heard God telling me that this was not the man I was going to marry. Furthermore, I didn't feel attracted to Ben at all. He was a very handsome guy, but I didn't have any desire to hold his hand, let alone (cringe) kiss him. When I paired what I felt like God was saying to me with the lack of romantic feelings I had for this really great guy, I came to the conclusion that I needed to end the relationship very quickly so as not to lead this guy on. Also, there was the fact that I had a baby. I didn't want Ben or Joseph to begin to love each other, just for me to break up with Ben later. It was then that I told God, "Well, God, You're sure not making this very easy on a girl. What am I supposed to tell the guy?! He hasn't done anything wrong. I'm going to feel like a complete jerk when I break up with him." And it was then that I asked for a favor from God. In a way, it was also my way of asking God for a sign as well as my way of passing the buck. I asked God to be the one to break things off between Ben and me. I didn't exactly know how God would handle the problem…I thought maybe He would have Ben break up with me instead; that way I wouldn't have to be the "bad guy." There was also the possibility that God would just continue to point me to the truth and then require me to put my big girl britches on and deal with this situation maturely. But what happened next was truly a sign to me that God *was* speaking to me after all, and that He had good plans for my baby boy and me. After that night that I had the conversation with God in which I asked for the "favor," Ben and I never spoke in person again. Ben never called me, and I never called him. We never had an argument or said any harsh words. We simply both went our separate ways without ever hearing from one another. Years later we reconnected through social media and are on friendly terms. Ben is now married, and he has a beautiful family!

To me, that was amazing! God truly is willing to walk you through this weird process of finding a partner—if that's the desire He has placed in your heart. He was willing to guide me every step of the way if I'd just listen. Plus, He also turned it into a learning process. I thought I was on the path to finding the right man, and while in a way I was, I was also on the path to becoming the woman God had called me to be. That was way more important anyway, even though I didn't realize it at the time. So time marched on, and my little baby boy was growing into a busy little guy. He began crawling and pulling himself up on furniture. Eventually he began walking and getting into everything! When Joseph turned one, I found a job and put the little guy in daycare. It was a very hard thing for me to do, but I was very thankful that I got what many single mothers do not get, which is to stay home with their baby for the whole first year of their baby's life. It still stung to have to send him to daycare, but it was something that had to be done.

I began working as a secretary at a local business. The hours were dependable, plus I got evenings and weekends off with the little guy. It was at this point that I decided to try out this Christian dating website, which is actually where I met my husband, Rene. It seems we've always been doing things differently. I knew I wanted to meet someone, and I knew I wanted for him to be a Christian, but there were just no young single men to be found anywhere in my small town (or at least it sure felt that way). I decided to create an online profile on this Christian dating website, and I still remember the day I saw Rene's profile. He messaged me first, and I called over the other girl who worked in the office with me, Denise. We stood together at my desk as I scrolled through and read aloud his profile information. I still even remember the picture he used as his profile pic. I remember his huge, gorgeous, almond-shaped brown eyes, and

I remember, after reading Denise the message he had sent me, saying these exact words to her with a dreamy, goofy, love-struck look in my eyes: "I could marry someone like him."

After corresponding with each other online for only a few days, Rene said to me, "If you're feeling brave, you could give me your phone number," as corny as that may sound. I guess I *was* feeling pretty brave because I did give him my number. That evening, he called me for the first time, and I think we basically spent the next four months living with phones glued to our heads. I remember going to work some days only having had a couple hours sleep. I knew I loved him, and I knew early on that I wanted to be with him forever. He was so risky and so different from anyone I had ever met. He dared to dream, and he was dreaming BIG with God. We read the Bible together on the phone and prayed together all the time. I would call him for advice. Honestly, I decided early on that I would give him my heart, and I knew beyond a shadow of a doubt that I would follow him anywhere. I didn't know what the future held for me and my little baby boy, but I felt like our future had Rene in it and that it was going to be amazing.

It didn't take long for Rene and me to know that we had to meet each other face to face like ASAP. Rene bought a ticket and rode to Sherman, Texas, from Phoenix, Arizona, on a Greyhound bus. My nanny has always been one of my closest friends, and so I divulged to her this online romance I had found. Well, to her generation, the Internet is some foreign, weird, and dangerous thing. In her mind, the Internet is where stalkers find their prey! At least that's the way it seemed at the time to her. She has actually warmed up to the Internet so much so that now she even has a Facebook account! It's hilarious, really—my grandma is on Facebook. She never tried to talk me out of meeting Rene, but I still remember how nervous it made her that I had found some guy online, was clearly in love and completely smitten with him, and was now going to go pick him up at a bus station so that he could stay a week with my family to meet everyone. She told me that just in case he turned out to be a psycho, Joseph should stay the night with her while I go to the bus stop to pick up "that guy from the Internet."

As I drove to Sherman to pick him up at the bus stop, I had this internal dialogue going on that went something like this: "This is amazing. I'm so excited. I finally get to meet him. Should I kiss him? Should I run into his arms? What should I do? What is appropriate? Should I even be doing this? Am I crazy? What if this is all some disgusting con? What if he's some sicko who wants to murder me and chop me into tiny pieces? What if it's a horrible prank and I wait at the bus stop for hours and he never shows? Oh God, I need to turn around. This is nuts." What an emotional rollercoaster! Welcome to my mind. So naturally, the smartest thing to do was to call my closest friend at the time, Shamanda. I needed some sound advice and a pep talk. I called her and began spewing out my frantic thoughts a million words a minute. Somehow she convinced me that everything was going to be okay and that I was going to be fine if I would stop thinking so much and just follow what God was telling me in my heart. All that great advice and I still felt only slightly calmer, but I definitely felt brave enough to see this thing through.

I still remember seeing that Greyhound bus unload. All the people poured out one by one, and when I finally saw him from afar, I had Shamanda on the phone. "Oh my God, oh my God, oh my God, Shamanda, I don't know what to do. I can't do this," I said to her, not taking a single breath in between words.

"Hang up the phone and go greet him, Amber. You can do this," she said.

I remember that when I first spotted him, I thought I would faint. I was afraid I would make a fool of myself, afraid he would be someone other than who I'd imagined him to be, and just in general I had the fear of the unknown. I got out of my car and started to awkwardly walk toward him. I was absolutely terrified. I bumbled ungracefully toward him, hoping he would see me first and recognize me. He did, and thankfully he met me in the middle of the parking lot, where we shared the first of many awkward, yet amazing kisses. Our kisses are a lot less awkward now, but they seem to be getting more amazeballs with time.

Rene met all my family while he was in town, and then he went back to Arizona on a Greyhound bus. I went to visit him once, and then shortly after, I went with him on a mission trip to Mexico. When I met Rene, he was acting as a translator, missionary, and intern to a ministry that organized mission trips into Mexico for churches. I went on one of the mission trips as a cook. My son Joseph, who was just a little over a year old at the time, stayed with my nanny while I was gone. She was only slightly less leery of "that guy from the Internet" at this point, and there was no way in God's green earth that she would have let me take her sweet baby Joseph out of the country. Who did I think I was, anyway? His momma or something?

This mission trip changed my life in a million different ways. Let me set the stage for you a little so you'll understand just how far this trip took me out of my comfort zone. I was born and raised in a small town. My whole life up until the age of twenty-one, I had never left my home state without one of my parents. I went to a little 2A country high school. I had never left the South, let alone the country. To say that I experienced culture shock in Mexico would be an understatement. During that season of my life, God was taking me out of my comfort zone and breaking the little country ideals I had formed in my mind about how "good Christians" lived and what they looked like. Also, I was delivered from materialism on this trip. Looking back, it's pretty funny, but at the time, I had never experienced anything quite like it. You see, I had no idea that when you fly on an airplane, your luggage has to stay under a certain weight. And let me tell you, my luggage was WAYYYYY over the weight limit. I had two bags, both of which were over the allowed weight for the standard checked baggage fee. I had been dropped off at the airport, and it seemed that I was just stuck. I was either going to have to pay hundreds of dollars to get my stuff there and back (not an option) or I was going to have to get rid of some stuff. About that time, I saw a girl who had on a uniform and clearly worked at the airport. She appeared to be a janitor. I explained my situation to her and asked her if she would either take some of my things or give them to someone who needed them. She reassured me that she knew someone in need, and she was very appreciative. So right there, in the middle of DFW Airport, I had to unpack my bags and throw about a third of my belongings into a clean trash bag. I mean, I didn't have to travel like a pauper after that (I still made sure I was gonna look very cute for my Rene), but I gave away so much of my things that it literally made me nauseated. After I got on the plane, I opened up my Bible and started reading. God guided me to Matthew 6:25-34:

> *Therefore I tell you, stop being perpetually uneasy (anxious and worried) about your life, what you shall eat or what you shall drink; or about your body, what you shall put on. Is not life greater [in quality] than food, and the body [far above and more excellent] than clothing? Look at the birds of the air; they neither sow nor reap nor gather into barns, and yet your heavenly Father*

keeps feeding them. Are you not worth much more than they? And who of you by worrying and being anxious can add one unit of measure (cubit) to his stature or to the span of his life? (Matthew 6:25-34 AMPC).

It dawned on me that I had been depending on those clothes and that stuff to impress Rene, but in reality, he was either going to love me for who I am or not at all. Just having that happen opened my eyes to how I really should just be myself, because if I'm pretending to be who I think Rene wants me to be or doing what I think will impress him, then how will I ever know if he truly loves me instead of just the image of me that I put on for him? This trip shook my world in every way imaginable. I met people there that were very different than the people around whom I grew up. Heck, RENE was very different than the people in the culture in which I grew up.

There is a unique and beautiful move of God on the inside of you that only you can release. Don't waste your time pretending to be someone else or trying to project a certain image because that is valuable time you could have been spending releasing His glory.

HOW SHOULD CHRISTIANS DATE?

For a second there, you might have thought I was about to give you a step-by-step manual that tells you precisely how Christians should or shouldn't date. Maybe you thought I would give you a list of restricting rules. Or maybe you're more like me so when you read that, it kind of ruffled your feathers because you thought I was about to boss you around. Well, I'm sure there are books out there that are ready to boss you around, make up dating rules for you, and give you "forty-three easy steps to date your boo and stay 'pure'," but I'm not much for telling people what to do. I like for people to use that thing that God put in between their ears called a brain and think for themselves. I would much rather equip you with information, tell you how to hear from the Holy Spirit (just ask and then listen), and let you figure out what's going to work for you in your life.

I will, however, be sharing some of the wisdom I have gained over the years. This is all wisdom I gained from doing things the wrong way (this accounts for almost half of my advice), wise counsel, or watching teens and young adults struggle through many broken hearts during the five years that I served as a youth pastor. Dating and purity are two of the biggest challenges that young Christians face, mainly because of some major misconceptions about it and because of the mindset by which it is often approached.

My adolescent years, long before I was saved or cared about anything like purity or Jesus, went something like this:

Met this boy. Oh, he's really cute. I hope he likes me. I think he likes me. Oh, wow, he likes me. We're going out. He could be the one. I'm so in love with him. I could never picture my life without him. I wanna be with him forever.... Two weeks later.... Wow, his breath stinks. It's annoying the way he follows me around at lunchtime. I'm gonna break up with him. Yay! I'm single...feels good!

At the football game I met this really hot guy. Oh wow, the way he looked at me made my heart skip a beat. He came right out and asked for my number. I gave it. We've been talking on the phone all night every night. We're going on a date this weekend. My mom thinks we're going to the movies, but his mom is out of town so we'll just go to his mom's house and hang out. I really love him. He's the sweetest guy I've ever met. We had a great date. We went all the way. It was so romantic. [Days later] Well, I haven't heard from him since our date.

Do you see a pattern here? The initial giddiness, the commit-ment to the other person (regardless of whether it was appropriate to be committed to this person on this level or whether they were equally committed), the spark, the passionate whirlwind of "love" followed by the dumping. **Sounds like a mini "marriage" (com-mitted relationship) ending in "divorce" (breakup).** And this is not uncommon. Based on my experience as a youth pastor, it's the common model for many young adult relationships. Many people are driven into this pattern of destructive behavior due to a root of self-hatred or a fear of rejection. Granted, those are not the only root causes, but my point is that they are looking for a better way. For too long Christians have simply rammed abstinence down people's throats without even thinking twice about empowering them with the knowledge of freedom by helping them to understand their worth and value to God.

This cycle that I just described will only lead to heartbreak, unhealthy soul ties, and deep wounds of the heart. Maybe a verse that describes the Father's best plan for "dating" is the verse below:

Treat younger men as brothers, older women as mothers, and younger women as sisters, with absolute purity (1 Timothy 5:1-2).

In other words, until you are married, treat members of the opposite sex as a sibling, *"with absolute purity"* (1 Tim. 5:2). This is what Rene and I have started to teach our children in regard to this matter.

When someone is dealing with sexual temptation or lustful thoughts, the problem is not an external one. The root problem lies somewhere in the heart, and it is a matter that the Holy Spirit longs to come in and help that person with by enabling him or her to receive healing in his or her heart. The Holy Spirit doesn't want to just cover up the root of the issue by placing safeguards and rules on you. That isn't real freedom anyway. Real freedom means dealing with this at the root so that you are free from the power of sin. Furthermore, if there's a root issue leading to impure thoughts, it won't be dealt with merely by getting married. The root issue will still be there, and it will just end up surfacing differently. It's much less complicated to deal with these root issues before marriage than it is to rush into a marriage just so you don't have to burn with lust. The thought may be, "Ahhh, let's just get married. It's a solution to our lust problem. Then our sex will be 'legal'." If there is a wound or hurt at the root of the lust issue, it won't just go away simply because you got married. Trust me on this one. I've lived this one out. Marriage doesn't solve the deeper issues of the heart. It magnifies them, if anything. For some, it magnifies the problems right away; for others, it may take longer and happen over time. But we have to deal with these things eventually, and it isn't hard to allow the Holy Spirit to bring healing to those painful places deep within our hearts. If you're willing, God can do more in five minutes than your therapist can do in five years of sessions. Don't think I'm advising you against therapy either. I'm just saying the Holy Spirit is like supernatural Neosporin, and if you'll ask Him, He'll come in like a healing balm and help you deal with the painful wounds deep inside of you. You may have hidden these things from people for years, but He knows you, He loves you, and He is not abandoning you to sort this out on your own.

My husband and I have been youth pastors for over five years, and sometimes I have felt like the kids at our church were my own. We have laughed together. We have cried together. We have journeyed together through some difficult heartbreaks and trials. Joseph is now nine years old, and one day he asked me why the magazines at the checkout line have pictures of women who are "almost naked," as he put it. The truth is that our kids are going to encounter women and men who are barely dressed, even at the beach. Do we teach them that to cover their eyes is the only possible way not to sin against this girl? Or do I teach my son that this girl in the fitness magazine is a harlot and that she is in sin (inferring to him that she is the one to blame for any temptation she might bring upon anyone else) because she is potentially causing others to lust? Well...unfortunately, many have decided these are our only options. This attitude impacts the way we view modesty, it impacts the way our Christian culture dates, and it impacts the way we view purity. But **I simply beg to differ that those are the only ways to view this. I do not believe these are our only options.** You are not an animal, driven by instincts and lust. You have control over your mind. You have the mind of Christ (see 1 Cor. 2:16). Self-control is one of the fruits of the Spirit (see Gal. 5:23). If one of my readers is having a problem with lustful thoughts or an addiction to pornography, I want you to know there is freedom for you. If you sin, it isn't someone else's fault; it is because of a lie you have believed. The anecdote is the truth. At this point I would like to recommend to you a book by Jonathan Welton called *Eyes of Honor: Training for Purity and Righteousness.* This book will take you even deeper on this subject matter. If you or someone you know is struggling with sexual sin, or even a pornography addiction, then I recommend this book. This is the only book on this topic that I've ever read that I do recommend, in fact, because many other books put a form of rules and legalism on people instead of leading them to freedom, which, I know, is Jonathan's heart. Another book that I have read that gives such a beautiful story and a tender heart on the matter of purity is a book called *Purity: The New Moral Revolution* by Kris Vallotton.

At one point, we lived in a neighborhood up in the mountains of Virginia, near West Virginia. It was beautiful, and though it was a neighborhood, it had a real country kind of feel, and our road got very little traffic. So the first thing my son set out to do was to scout out the neighborhood to find some kids with whom he could play. Oh, and that he did—he hit the mother lode. As it turns out, he met a couple of little girls who were the same age as him. They were cute as a button, and he would play with them for hours on end. Well, one day I went for a walk with my son, and I stopped to say hi to the little girls. One of the girls pranced out to the edge of her yard. "Ummm, I just think you should know," she said with her hand on her hips, "that SHEEEE (pointing to the other little girl) has a crush on your son. And basically I do too. We all do." As we continued on our walk, my son asked me what a crush was. I explained to him that it was when a boy/girl found another boy/girl to be cute. We were just having a casual conversation about it all since he had brought it up. This was definitely not me lecturing him. These are the teachable moments. I've found that my kids really want to know these things, and when they ask us, we have an open door into their hearts. We went on to talk about how God designed us to be attracted to members of the opposite sex. It's normal to think, "She's pretty" or, "He's handsome," which, I think, was the girl's intention—to communicate that she thought Joseph was handsome. As his mom, I would have to agree; he's a pretty good-looking kid. This conversation led us to talk about boyfriends and girlfriends, and I asked him his thoughts on girlfriend/boyfriend relationships. I didn't have to remind him of the Scripture that will guide him as to how he should treat all girls (1 Tim. 5:1-2) because it's just been something about which we've always talked openly, but it's exactly what he mentioned. I was really impressed, though—not because he remembered the exact appropriate Scripture verse and not because he could recite the verse back to me, because that wasn't the case either, but rather because he remembered the application of it. And he didn't feel like the type of girlfriend/boyfriend relationship in which some of the kids he knew were participating was honoring both partners in the way that he knew was appropriate. **This Scripture, First Timothy 5:1-2, offers him a filter for a variety of situations. When Joseph feels like he has been placed in a compromising situation with a young woman, he can ask himself, "Is this protecting her? Am I treating her (even in my thoughts, which I have control over) just as I would treat my sister?"**

I mention this conversation that Joseph and I had only to show how teaching our children about purity, dating, sex, and some of the harder topics doesn't really have to be that hard. We can start small and build upon these concepts like building blocks when life opens the door to that conversation. When children are curious and receptive, they ask us the hard questions. They want to know more, and that's our chance to teach them, a little at a time.

It is true that there are many people around the world who would find it common and acceptable to live together and have sex before marriage in order to "test each other out" to see if they'll be able to tolerate each other once married, or to see if they're a good fit for one another. In other words, they are living as a married couple for a period of time to see if they like being married to one another. It might sound logical, but the problem with that is that it is fornication, and statistically, just by living together before marriage, they are increasing their odds of divorce (if they ever get married). Furthermore, what if that's someone else's future wife/husband with whom he/she is having sex? Is there not a better way to figure out if this is the person God has called you to marry? I truly believe God wants to walk us through this process. The Holy Spirit is ready and willing to speak wisdom to those who will seek Him and listen.

We must ask ourselves the following question: What's the purpose behind my dating? I think many people would agree that the point of dating is to get to know another person in order to see if that person is the spouse that God created for you. Once I became married, the point of dating for me became to deepen our relationship, to have fun together, and to keep our romance alive.

Surely there's a better way to get to know someone and find out if that's the spouse God intended for you than to create unhealthy soul ties and to open yourself up to heartbreak by engaging in sex and other sex acts and by fostering intimacy—basically, by treating members of the opposite sex in a way that you wouldn't treat your brother or sister. What I've seen very often is teens and adults alike dating in a way that seems a lot like practicing for marriage and divorce by repeating the intimacy/separation cycle multiple times with different boyfriends/girlfriends.

I have been sharing these ideas with my son as he would ask questions and as the opportunity would present itself for a couple of years now. My other children are girls, ages five and three, and I plan on having the same types of conversations with them, like the one I had with my son, when it's natural and when the opportunity presents itself. The reason I do this is because I think that this should be a normal thing that we talk about with our sons and daughters, even from a young age. Trust me, you don't want to wait until your daughter has fainted in her bathroom because she started her menstrual cycle and thinks she is dying. That is literally what happened to me, except I didn't faint; I just yelled loudly until my mom came into the bathroom.

I also believe television shows have greatly impacted our cultural ideas of dating and what is considered godly or honoring. And if you don't believe me, go watch TeenNick or the Disney Channel in the afternoons. The teens are in committed relationships with each other where they fall in love, sometimes make out, and often break up. They're not looking for a potential spouse (not that I'm saying that we should be driven by that), and they're certainly not treating members of the opposite sex in an honoring way as if they were their brother/sister.

I'm not suggesting at all that television causes people to sin, but when the television relationships begin to define what real-life relationships are supposed to look like, then that becomes a problem. We actually don't have cable or satellite at all anymore. Rene and I haven't had it for most of our married life. We made the decision years ago when we began paying off our debt. And then one day, I noticed something very innocent and different about my children, especially when we would occasionally watch television programs at other people's houses and they would gasp in shock at some of the rude things kids would say on shows. It's not that we're trying to shelter them from "the evils of the world"—because they're still randomly exposed to these shows, whether it be at someone's house, a restaurant with a television, etc.—but the main point here is that we can't let our ideas and beliefs about dating be DEFINED by these shows or other ungodly sources. Children shouldn't be TRAINED by television, movies, books, or other sources of popular culture. When we accept what the media presents as a normal idea of what a healthy relationship looks like, whether we realize it or not, we have allowed ourselves to be trained and taught about healthy relationships by popular culture.

I'm afraid that unfortunately, a lot of the dating advice that the Church has given in the past has been religious and legalistic, which has caused many people to look elsewhere for advice, including television shows and other forms of popular culture. Some Christians have decided that instead of tackling the actual flaw with dating, we should just abandon the act of dating and trade it for something more structured and supervised. The real problem here is a posture of the heart and possibly a misunderstanding of what purity is all about. What has happened is that well-meaning people have seen the same flaws that I see in how dating is sometimes practiced and have decided that the best way to protect their children and teens is to add rules and "accountability." On a side note here, I'm not at all opposed to accountability. The problem arises when someone substitutes requiring chaperones for addressing the real issue, which is in the heart.

I'm actually not here to tell you how to date, even though I've included here in my book a chapter on dating. I don't have a dating model to offer you. Nor have I come here trying to persuade you to try courting instead. It's my personal opinion that different things work for different people and we all have to find our own way. Part of the very good news is that you're not alone. The Holy Spirit is with you, and He will give you advice, speak to you, nudge you, and help you make the best choices. Whether you decide to say you're dating, or even if you say you're going to try courting, invite the Holy Spirit into the center of that relationship and allow Him to be the tour guide. Use your mind (because remember, you have the mind of Christ), and partner with the Holy Spirit (see 1 Cor. 2:16). You guys will make a great team. Get inner healing if you have some issues in your heart that are keeping you from walking in purity. I believe we are called to transform the dating culture of the Church and of our society. That will happen when we are being led by the Holy Spirit and when we talk more openly about the issues we face along the way without fear and without people trying to control other people with their traditions or rules. Talk openly with the people in your life who you know you can trust. If you don't have anyone like that in your life, then pray and ask God to send someone. It might not happen the next day, but He is faithful and He will send that person in good time.

I've found that in Christian circles, there is apparently this big ongoing debate between dating versus courting. If you hear the courting camp talk, dating is painted like this option with no boundaries, whereas they describe courting as "safe" because it has rules, guidelines, and accountability to keep the young 'uns from screwing up their lives. Can I please insert my two cents here? What if it's deeper than that? What if rules upon rules aren't the answer? What if the answer lies in the posture of our heart and in what we believe? Multiple times, the Bible makes it very clear that in the New Covenant, of which we are partakers in Christ, that the law is now written on our hearts. Second Corinthians 3:1-6 reinforces this. Jeremiah 31:33 prophesies that the New Covenant would be different in that God would write the law on our hearts. Hebrews 10:16 proclaims the fulfillment of Jeremiah 31:33 through Christ. Romans 2:15 says that even the Gentiles of that time demonstrated that God's law is written in their hearts for their own conscience.

We can read in the Bible where it says that under the Old Covenant, the heart was deceitfully wicked and couldn't be trusted (see Jer. 17:9). Many Christians still believe that is true for them, even under the New Covenant, and that is why they feel the need to have external rules imposed on them. It feels safer to them. They do not believe they can trust themselves. It is not true for us in the New Covenant, though. In the new and better covenant, we have the mind of Christ (see 1 Cor. 2:16). In the new and better covenant of which we are partakers, we are clothed in the righteousness of Christ (see Rom. 5:17). We are a new creation, no longer with a heart of stone but with a heart of flesh (see 2 Cor. 5:17; Ezek. 11:19; 36:26).

In the Old Covenant, God led His people externally. There were prophets to come speak the Word of the Lord, whether it be correction or instruction. But listen to this verse in Hebrews that compares the New Covenant to the old Mosaic Covenant:

> *For if there had been nothing wrong with that first covenant, no place would have been sought for another. But God found fault with the people and said: "The days are coming, declares the Lord, when I will make a new covenant with the people of Israel and with the people of Judah. It will not be like the covenant I made with their ancestors when I took them by the hand to lead them out of Egypt, because they did not remain faithful to My covenant, and I turned away from them, declares the Lord. This is the covenant I will establish with the people of Israel after that time, declares the Lord. I will put My laws in their minds and write them on their hearts* (Hebrews 8:7-10).

From this verse (and others) we see that God's heart for His people is that each of us would have personal relationship with Him and that we would be governed from the inside. How will that happen? God Himself has taken up residence on the inside of you. If God lives within you, like First Corinthians 3:16 says, then He will lead us and guide us to walk in love and release His glory in our lives through all that we do.

> *Don't you know that you yourselves are God's temple and that God's Spirit dwells in your midst?* (1 Corinthians 3:16).

I don't mean to say that it's just you and God and you don't need anybody else. I firmly believe in wise counsel. The point I'm trying to make here is that ultimately I can't hand you a rulebook, and neither can anyone else. Your journey is going to look different than anyone else's. You need the accountability of friends, family, and loved ones in your life, but you need to be led by God as well.

WHAT DOES BIBLICAL ACCOUNTABILITY LOOK LIKE IN THE NEW COVENANT?

I have to be really honest with you here. I used to hate hearing and talking about accountability. But really, the problem was what my idea of what accountability was, because I had this image in my head that having accountability was basically like having a tattletale in your life who would go tell your pastor on you if you started acting stupid—either that or someone who would call you out on anything that he or she didn't feel like you should be doing. This is actually probably a commonly accepted definition of what many people think of as accountability.

Can I propose something slightly different here? I've come to see that what I used to believe about accountability is totally lame and not really very helpful at all. Allow me to explain. In Christ, I am a new creation (see 2 Cor. 5:17). Completely new. So if I do something sinful, risky, or un-Christlike, then I'm acting out of character. Who I really am—my true identity—is God's princess, Amber. I am who God says I am, and He says I'm pure, I'm clothed in righteousness, that I have the mind of Christ, and that I am seated in heavenly places (see Rom. 5:17; 1 Cor. 2:16; Eph. 2:6). If I have participated in behavior that doesn't represent who I am, my true identity in Christ, then perhaps I need someone to remind me who I really am. Of course, we do have the Holy Spirit to convict us of our righteousness, but think about how encouraging it would be to have someone in your life who is brave enough to step in and say, "You are capable of so much more. Come back over here and remember who you really are, who God says you are." Accountability should be less like a pointing finger and more like a loving fellow soldier linking arms with you.

I want to share with you an analogy that I heard Dr. Jonathan Welton explain during a lecture at the school he founded, Welton Academy. These are not his words verbatim because I typed up what he was saying as fast as possible during a class. I gained his permission to share this analogy:

Dr. Jekyll and Mr. Hyde.

Before you got saved, you were like Dr. Jekyll and Mr. Hyde. The story goes that Dr. Jekyll has these desires to do evil things so he creates a potion that transforms him into a different-looking person so that he can go out and do evil deeds and then change back into his real self, Dr. Jekyll.

Many Christians would even be willing to say they can relate to that story in their own lives, and unfortunately there are many Christians who fully believe this is actually a very true depiction of life. Here's a better analogy to describe to you what actually happens once you become saved:

One day, Jesus comes and knocks on the door of Dr. Jekyll's (that's you) house. Dr. Jekyll answers the door. "Hi, Jesus. Nice to meet You. Please come in. We'd love to have You come in here and live with us."

Jesus says, "Hang on, Dr. Jekyll. I've got to take care of something first."

Jesus snatches up Mr. Hyde, takes him down the road and to a hill called Mount Calvary, and Mr. Hyde is crucified with Christ.

Dead. Gone. Finished. The only ones left alive are Dr. Jekyll and Jesus.

BUT...Dr. Jekyll's home is still full of Mr. Hyde's stuff.

Mr. Hyde's old Xbox games still line the shelves of the entertainment center, and so do his movies. The mp3 player still has Mr. Hyde's playlists, and all over the walls is Mr. Hyde's art.

Dr. Jekyll begins to clear out Mr. Hyde's stuff. The first day, Dr. Jekyll calls one of those waste management companies to bring out a huge dumpster, and Dr. Jekyll fills it with round after round of Mr. Hyde's stuff.

Dr. Jekyll has the dumpster hauled off, relieved that all that stuff is finally gone. He starts hanging his own beautiful art on the walls and buying colorful new curtains for the windows. One day, Dr. Jekyll heads to the attic to find a ladder, and he finds boxes of Mr. Hyde's stuff. Mr. Hyde has been dead and gone for months now, but this box of his junk was in the attic all along. Dr. Jekyll gladly loads the boxes in the back of his pickup truck to drive it to the dump.

One day, Dr. Jekyll is vacuuming, and Jesus whispers, "Look under the bed."

Dr. Jekyll looks under the bed to find some old magazines of Mr. Hyde's left there. Dr. Jekyll gets a trash bag and throws them away.

You see, Jesus doesn't come in and magically make all of Mr. Hyde's stuff disappear. That certainly would be a lot easier, but what He does do is partner with you. Because He partners with us like that, it builds our faith and deepens our relationship with Him as we're "cleaning house," so to speak.

Here's what is true of you once you became born again:

- He gives you the mind of Christ (see 1 Cor. 2:16).

- He gives you a heart of flesh to replace the heart of stone (see Ezek. 11:19; 36:26).

- He says to you that your own righteousness was like filthy rags, which is why He wants to clothe you in His, so that you may reign in life (see Rom. 5:17). You're now clothed in the righteousness of Christ.

- You had a sin nature (Mr. Hyde), but now you're a partaker of the divine nature (see 2 Pet. 1:4).

- You are empowered to clean Mr. Hyde's stuff out of your own house.

Just because you find some of Mr. Hyde's shirts in the closet doesn't mean he's still living there or that he has come back. Mr. Hyde is gone, and you need to remind yourself of that.

When we realize that we have the Spirit of God living inside of us, ready and willing to communicate with us, we don't need other people to create rules for us. We just need to connect with His Spirit and learn how to hear His voice. We get better at this over time. He will speak from the inside of your heart, where He lives. God speaks in different ways at different times. Sometimes God's voice will come through visions or dreams. Sometimes it will take the form of a still, small voice or even an audible voice (see 1 Kings 19:12). But taking the time to listen each day, as well as reading your Bible, will help you discern what He is saying to you. God cares about your dating journey. He cares about you and will help guide you through the difficult decisions of life where there is no black-and-white answer spelled out in Scripture. He can be your very best friend. When you realize that and really embrace Him as such, that lonely ache will go away, which helps you to make choices based off of what He says and what you believe is best, rather than the emotions of desperation and loneliness.

Chapter 7

SUBMISSION IN MARRIAGE

I know, I know...I've said the dreaded s-word. I'm sorry (not sorry). My hope is that if that word makes you cringe, this chapter will allow you to see it in a new light. I, too, hated this word for a long time, but I don't now, and that's pretty freeing. In fact, when you saw that word here, if you cringed, I don't blame you. I don't even blame you if you considered putting down this book. Good teaching in the Church regarding submission in marriage (or just submission in general) has been almost nonexistent, but it IS surfacing, so be encouraged. If you wanted to know more about submission or how to submit so you started researching the books or teachings that are out there, what you would find, predominantly, is teaching that instructs women to submit to their men. You'll read all about how if you'll submit to your husband, God will bless you and bless your marriage. You will read all about how you're just supposed to pray for your husband and keep your mouth shut, and how this magical thing called submission is going to make your marriage wonderful. That is NOT what I'm about to tell you.

Submission is a huge part of marriage, but I know for a fact that my Bible talks about submission in a very different way than how I was taught and how the vast majority of Christians are being taught by the Church. My Bible talks about a very different form of submission than that which was modeled for me throughout my childhood and adolescence.

There are two different ways to read your Bible:

1.   You can read your Bible in a way that lets God teach you His nature, His ways, and His heart and that allows the Holy Spirit to reveal to you what God is saying along the way.

2.   You can read your Bible in a way that involves trying to prove and back up what you already believe. In this case, you probably have all your favorite verses that reinforce your belief system highlighted and underlined, while you neglect certain chapters or verses because you don't quite know how to fit them into what you already believe.

In order to explain submission, I want to start by telling you the story about how I came to understand what it really means and what the Bible really says about it. I was raised with the idea that men are in charge and that the godly thing for women to do is submit. This caused me a lot of heartache, as I struggled internally with this belief system. Sometimes I felt that I was wrestling with my own self. On the one hand, all I wanted was to be a quiet, meek, submissive Christian wife. And on the other hand, I had differing opinions than my husband. I had ideas. I had dreams. I had goals. The very painful truth is that in many Christian circles, women like me are labeled "Jezebels" or "rebellious." Women like me who are strong and bold are often painted in a villainous light. If you are a woman who is bold and strong—you have ideas, dreams, differing opinions, and an outgoing personality—I want you to let go of what other people have said about you. Forgive them. They only viewed you in that light because of a faulty belief system. Many people, including myself, have just decided to believe what they've been told by other people or by tradition rather than actually being students of the Bible and looking for themselves to see what the Word of God says.

I want to start kind of at the beginning of my marriage so you can know where I'm coming from.

I've heard a lot of people talk about this blissful thing called a "honeymoon phase" that occurs right after getting married. According to what I've been told, it's this period of time after getting married that's all mushy-gushy and romantic and nothing can go wrong. Many people apparently experience this, based off of what I've heard. Well...we didn't. We experienced something commonly known as a "reality check." My dad had warned me about this before. He warned me that the whole time you're dating, the only thing the other person is showing you is the best version of themselves, but then when you are married, they expose their real self, and they may not be as "picture perfect" as when the two of you were just dating. It's kind of strange that I never took my dad seriously when he would say this, but I later found out the truth of his words the hard way.

There were so many reasons why our first several years of marriage were the hardest—and I mean they were hard. I got pregnant a month after we were married, and three months after we were married, Rene accepted a position as youth pastor at a church that was five hours away from my hometown. In the beginning, the arguments and bad days far outnumbered the good days. I cried a lot because marriage wasn't what I had dreamed of. I felt that he definitely didn't pursue me like he had before we got married. On top of that, I had many spiritual and emotional issues that God was allowing to be brought to the surface so that I would let Him heal me... and it was a very ugly combination. I was wounded from my past, I was not feeling loved or desired, and I was both spiritually immature and just plain old immature. My husband had many of the same problems when it came to immaturity and spiritual immaturity. He had also been hurt deeply in the past and was working through that. He just didn't know *how* to express love in a healthy way at the time. At one point during my pregnancy, just looking for someone to point me to a solution, when I went to the doctor I bared my soul to him. Maybe I was just in need of a friend; I don't know. But the doctor put me on an antidepressant, and I had some really awful reactions to it. I felt like I was just angry all the time because of the medicine. It seemed to stir up more fights, to the point where we couldn't even be around each other for two minutes without arguing. One day, in a blind rage, I took my medicine the doctor had given me and I flushed it down the toilet. You're not really supposed to do that, though, because it was the kind of medicine you're supposed to taper off of. However, I didn't care. I had flushed it, and that was that. I really don't recommend that anyone else do that, but this shows the severity of the anger and hopelessness that I felt at the time.

We had a lot of problems through which we had to work. We both needed a lot of inner healing. We both had issues galore. But one of the huge issues we had that I believe others can benefit from hearing about is the following: my strong will. There was this ongoing power struggle in our relationship. As a matter of fact, about a year after getting married, we started going to marital counseling with a friend of ours, who was also a local pastor. Pastor Bob (not his real name) gave us this very long personality test, where we had to fill in the bubbles. Next week when we came back, he had the results and he told us what our personality tests had revealed. We were extreme opposites across the board, except for one thing: we are both extremely dominant personalities. "In fact," Pastor Bob told us, "if y'all weren't already married, I would have advised against it. What's done is done though...."

Well, that didn't sound like a lot of hope to me. I had an aversion to being controlled, and I just wanted to be loved for who I was. At the time, I definitely felt that Rene had a control issue (hey, so did I. I can admit that) and didn't know how to express love. That, my friends, is how you spell "toxic." We both were fighting to "be the boss," and it was not a pretty sight. I wish that I could tell you that a couple years later we worked it all out and we were just fine as frog's hair, but I can't. The truth is that we struggled for many years, and only in the last few years has it gotten better. We just celebrated our seventh anniversary this past September, and I can honestly tell you that for the first time in our lives we really are starting to learn how to enjoy each other. We are finding our groove. We have learned how to love each other, and we are still learning how to love one another.

I want to rewind our story just a little bit for you, back to when we were going to counseling with Pastor Bob. Once we identified that we both were people with control issues, we did what any logical Christians would do: we tried to break my dominant little spirit. Not Rene's...mine. Because when a man has control issues, for some reason, much of the Christian community does not seem to have a problem with it. It's perceived as normal. Of course—he's supposed to be the big boss, the head honcho. Doesn't the Bible say that men are in charge and their wives need to submit and do everything they say? Well, that was my interpretation of it at the time, so I viewed myself as flawed. That's what I had been taught to believe, and it was the example I had seen play out in front of me in numerous couples. It sure seemed like it was going to make my husband one happy camper. So that's all there was to it. I just needed to put on my big girl britches, find a way to break my strong spirit, shut my brain off, and submit. I felt like a train was coming and I was preparing to let it hit me. I started reading books on the issue, and looking back now, I'm so glad those books didn't change me. I'm so glad they didn't break my strong spirit. I didn't know it then, but my personality, including my wild and strong spirit, is a gift from the Father. It's who He created me to be.

But why does much of the Christian community have this strange idea that men are supposed to be the ones in charge, calling all the shots—"the big boss"—while women are supposed to learn to submit to whatever their husbands say, whether it's right or wrong? That's what I want to talk about. It is actually scripturally based—or rather, I should say it's based on a couple of verses taken out of historical context. So let's take a look at where this idea comes from.

Submit to one another out of reverence for Christ. **Wives, submit yourselves to your own husbands as you do to the Lord. For the husband is the head of the wife as Christ is the head of the church, His body, of which He is the Savior. Now as the church submits to Christ, so also wives should submit to their husbands in everything.** *Husbands, love your wives, just as Christ loved the church and gave Himself up for her to make her holy, cleansing her by the washing with water through the word, and to present her to Himself as a radiant church, without stain or wrinkle or any other blemish, but holy and blameless. In this same way,* *husbands ought to love their wives as their own bodies. He who loves his wife loves himself* (Ephesians 5:21-28).

Okay, now as you'll notice, I bolded one little section. That's where this idea comes from. I've heard a lot of different viewpoints on this topic because I read a lot of books about breaking a woman's strong will and learning to submit, as a result of my struggle in the early years of my marriage. I've even seen people attempt to redefine the word *submit* just to make this whole ordeal a little less ugly and unlikable. Basically, in the original Greek translations, the word *submit* means "to be subject to." There's no way around what the word actually means, but I want to share something that may really open your eyes when you read the whole portion of Scripture that I provided for you:

SUBMISSION SHOULD BE SOMETHING THAT GOES BOTH WAYS IN A MARRIAGE.

I hope that didn't shock you too badly there, because honestly, seven years ago, if I had read that in a book, I would have closed it and assumed that person was deceived. But I'm not deceived. It's right there, spelled out for us in Scripture in verse 21 (the one we all skip). Let us look at the whole passage of Scripture again:

Submit to one another out of reverence for Christ. Wives, submit yourselves to your own husbands as you do to the Lord. For the husband is the head of the wife as Christ is the head of the church, His body, of which He is the Savior. Now as the church submits to Christ, so also wives should submit to their husbands in everything.

Husbands, love your wives, just as Christ loved the church and gave Himself up for her to make her holy, cleansing

*her by the washing with water through the word, and to
present her to Himself as a radiant church, without stain
or wrinkle or any other blemish, but holy and blameless.
In this same way, husbands ought to love their wives as
their own bodies. He who loves his wife loves himself*
(Ephesians 5:21-28).

In a marriage, we should submit to one another. Things should
be give-and-take. If only one party is doing all the submitting, then
there's no balance, and that person wouldn't be submitting to the
other out of reverence for Christ, as the bolded portion of Scripture
above asks us to do. During the time in which Ephesians was written, this was revolutionary. This passage of Scripture was liberating
for women and not oppressive, not like it is used now. So why do
people use this Scripture selectively like they do?

Well, part of the reason this happens is because of where
the chapter break is located and where the title heading is placed.
Depending on what Bible version you're reading, there may be a title
heading in between verses 21 and 22. Now I want to tell you something that some of you may already know, but when I realized this
for the first time, it was somewhat of a surprise to me. It was one of
those "Aha!" moments, where suddenly things clicked into place and
I could understand. In the oldest manuscripts of the Scriptures that
we now call the Bible, there were no chapter titles or even numbered
verses. These were all added later in order to make the verses easier to
locate and reference. Now, that makes sense to me that it would be
a lot easier to reference a verse if there is a number and chapter with
which to associate a line of text, but these documents were originally
not broken up. Many of them were letters and were meant to be read
from beginning to end. They were certainly not meant to be broken
apart and used selectively, which is how many people use verse 22.

It's a big problem when someone decides to pluck one verse out and nail someone else with it to try to make him or her do what that person wants. That is not healthy. The Bible has to be taken as a whole. It makes sense as a whole. The Bible balances itself and explains itself as a whole. Taking one Scripture out and not considering it in light of the entire book as a whole is confusing. And most of the time when a person does this, that person is trying to justify a belief system, instead of reading the Bible and to be taught by the Bible itself and by Holy Spirit.

Just because the Bible doesn't specifically spell it out in that passage of Scripture that husbands should also obey their wives doesn't mean it isn't God's will. That is skewed logic. Let's use that same skewed logic to look at a different portion of that Scripture. When we do, I think you'll start to realize with me just how ridiculous that skewed logic is.

> *Submit to one another out of reverence for Christ. Wives, submit yourselves to your own husbands as you do to the Lord. For the husband is the head of the wife as Christ is the head of the church, His body, of which He is the Savior. Now as the church submits to Christ, so also wives should submit to their husbands in everything.* **Husbands, love your wives,** *just as Christ loved the church and gave Himself up for her to make her holy, cleansing her by the washing with water through the word, and to present her to Himself as a radiant church, without stain or wrinkle or any other blemish, but holy and blameless. In this same way,* **husbands ought to love their wives as their own bodies. He who loves his wife loves himself** (Ephesians 5:21-28).

This time the emphasis is on the "husbands love your wives" part. Well, that portion of Scripture does not tell wives that they must love their husbands. So, using the skewed logic that many people use with verse 22, should I then come to the conclusion that it isn't God's will that wives should love their husbands? Some of y'all are thinking I'm nuts to say that. Of course the Bible says in other places that LOVE goes both ways, so you can't just take that verse and assume the love only goes one way—except that's what people have done with verse 22. They don't quote verse 21; they pretend like it doesn't exist. Instead, they pluck that one verse out, verse 22, and use it to control others.

It is not God's will that people be controlled by other people. It is His desire that people would have self-control and be led by Holy Spirit.

> *Wives, in the same way submit yourselves to your own husbands so that, if any of them do not believe the word, they may be won over without words by the behavior of their wives, when they see the purity and reverence of your lives. Your beauty should not come from outward adornment, such as elaborate hairstyles and the wearing of gold jewelry or fine clothes. Rather, it should be that of your inner self, the unfading beauty of a gentle and quiet spirit, which is of great worth in God's sight. For this is the way the holy women of the past who put their hope in God used to adorn themselves.* **They submitted themselves to their own husbands, like Sarah, who obeyed Abraham and called him her lord.** *You are her daughters if you do what is right and do not give way to fear. Husbands, in the same way be considerate as you live with your wives, and treat them with respect as the weaker partner and as heirs with you of the gracious gift of life, so that nothing will hinder your prayers* (1 Peter 3:1-7).

Much of the time, when submission is being taught, the verse Ephesians 5:22 is brought up (alone, of course, and not accompanied by verse 21), along with this passage in First Peter 3. The premise is that all women should be obedient and submissive to their husbands just like Sarah. Now remember what we talked about earlier—about the whole Bible being taken as a whole? Well, to me, Paul's instruction in Ephesians 5:21 is enough all on its own to say that submission goes both ways. But I realized something very interesting one day when I was reading about Abraham and Sarah, who are referenced here in verse 5 of the First Peter 3 passage. I bolded it for you in the passage above. What if I told you that Abraham and Sarah practiced mutual submission? What if I told you there was a time when God Himself spoke to Abraham and told him to obey his wife on a particular matter? Let's just go there.

You can find the entire story in Genesis 16. Sarah and Abraham had been given a promise by God that their descendants would be so numerous that they would outnumber the sand on a seashore and the stars in the sky, but Sarah was barren and they were both very old. The promise seemed impossible; and so, Sarah and Abraham did what many of us have done: they began to brainstorm as to how they could make this promise happen on their own. Sarah has this (very bad) idea that she could give Abraham her handmaiden, Hagar, so that Hagar can conceive a child on her behalf. When it comes time for Hagar to give birth, she can birth on top of Sarah, and, therefore, the child will be Sarah's. This was a common practice actually, and to Sarah at the time, this might have been considered the "next best thing" to giving birth herself. But, as you might imagine, this doesn't end well and it causes terrible resentment between Sarah and Hagar, and also between Sarah and Abraham. In fact, even though it was Sarah's terrible idea (but a common practice of that day), she blames

Abraham in Genesis 16:5. Hagar does become pregnant and gives birth to a son named Ishmael. Time marches on, and fourteen years later, God is faithful to His promise: Sarah does conceive, and she gives birth to Isaac. Imagine that. God was faithful to His promise, and He didn't need Sarah and Abraham's help to cause those promises to come to pass. Here's the deal. As you can imagine, the situation with Hagar and Ishmael is not ideal. Can you imagine the tension and resentment there might have been? Let's read Genesis 21:

> *The child grew and was weaned, and on the day Isaac was weaned Abraham held a great feast. But Sarah saw that the son whom Hagar the Egyptian had borne to Abraham was mocking, and she said to Abraham, "Get rid of that slave woman and her son, for that woman's son will never share in the inheritance with my son Isaac." The matter distressed Abraham greatly because it concerned his son. But God said to him, "Do not be so distressed about the boy and your slave woman. Listen to whatever Sarah tells you, because it is through Isaac that your offspring will be reckoned. I will make the son of the slave into a nation also, because he is your offspring." Early the next morning Abraham took some food and a skin of water and gave them to Hagar. He set them on her shoulders and then sent her off with the boy. She went on her way and wandered in the Desert of Beersheba (Genesis 21:8-14).*

So clearly here in Scripture we see that Abraham and Sarah had a relationship of mutual submission. God specifically tells Abraham to do as Sarah is saying to do, even though this whole debacle all came to pass because she insisted that Abraham have a child with Hagar.

I'm not trying to paint Sarah in a bad light here so that you'll think badly of her or anything, but a lot of times when I hear people quote First Peter 3:1-6, they are acting like Sarah was this perfect model for the quiet, obedient little woman who just listened to her man and did as she was told. Sarah is a lot like every other woman on the face of the earth. She made mistakes. She sometimes doubted the promises of God and tried to figure things out on her own. She took her frustration out on her husband and ended up blaming him for a mess she made. But look how she is remembered in Scripture. It's actually pretty encouraging to me because Sarah isn't some perfect woman who never messed up. It would seem that like Abraham, Sarah, too, believed in the Lord, and it was credited to her as righteousness. Scripture doesn't come right out and say that, but in Genesis 15:6 it does say that about Abraham; and the New Testament writers held both Sarah and Abraham in high esteem.

WHAT I'M NOT SAYING

I want to stop here and take a moment to explain what I'm not saying. What I'm not saying is that women should dominate their men and boss them around. I'm NOT saying that women should make their husbands submit to them.

I remember in my early years of marriage hearing a friend of Rene's talking about how he finally got his wife to submit to him. He talked about how he didn't give her any choice but to obey him because he said that if she didn't, their marriage would be over. This is wrong. That is emotional abuse, and I would say that whether it was the man doing it or the woman doing it. Submission, just like love, is a choice. Without a choice, it is domination, not submission.

For a marriage to thrive, it takes two people who are willing to submit to one another, as it says in Ephesians 5:21. Love is about preferring another person over yourself. You cannot force someone to submit to you, and even if you could, then it wouldn't be love. Love brings freedom. Love is a choice. Love wouldn't be love if there wasn't the freedom to make choices. Submission will happen naturally in a marriage in which both people love each other and put God at the center of their marriage.

This September, my husband and I will celebrate our eighth wedding anniversary. I think we are really starting to thrive and enjoy one another. I now am able to hold my head high, look in the mirror, and know that I AM a submissive wife. And that doesn't mean I don't have a voice or that my husband dominates me. Sometimes I submit to him. Sometimes he submits to me. Remember when I told you about that personality test we had taken during marriage counseling? At the time, we thought it was a bad thing that we were extremely different than each other and only shared the tendency to be dominating. Being a dominating person is not necessarily a good thing, but the fact that we are polar opposites in every other way turned out to be a good thing. For example, my husband is the most impulsive and spontaneous person I've ever met, whereas I like to look forward to things in advance. He tends to be more impulsive when making a decision, while I will deliberate on a thing and gather information about it until the day of the deadline. We balance each other out because if it weren't for him, I'd never commit to a decision on anything, and without me, he'd never be able to plan more than two days in advance. I like to be early to everything, and when we were newlyweds, if he made us late anywhere I would cry the whole way there. I needed to chill out and realize that being late isn't the end of the world. He needed to learn that being on time is necessary in order to be trusted by other people, especially if you're a leader. We balanced each other out in this, and now, most of the time, we're on time, but if we're late, I'm pretty chill about it because I know that sometimes being late is unavoidable. I could literally go on and on and on for pages about all the ways we balance each other out.

My husband and I come to the "table" with different talents and strengths, as does every other married couple out there. I manage our family calendar because Rene easily forgets appointments. Since he's weaker in this area, I carry the weight and "take the lead" in the area of family calendar planning. I keep a calendar posted in the kitchen so he can see what's coming up, and as long as he tells me about his speaking engagements or appointments, they'll be on that calendar. On the other hand, my husband is really good at haggling prices and getting a good bargain if we're shopping around for something. So when it comes to things like getting a good deal on a house, I completely pull back and heavily rely on him to take the lead.

LEADING LIKE JESUS

When it boils down to it, a husband and wife are two people who are leading together. A Christian husband and wife are two people who should both be Christlike. That means we resemble Jesus. Especially when a couple already has children, it's important for a husband and wife to see themselves as teammates. When one wins, they both win. When we make it a point to lead like Jesus, everyone wins. Jesus never manipulated people to support His plan. With Jesus, you either followed or you didn't. He also wasn't so stubborn that He couldn't change His mind or hear from others. In fact, His very first miracle wasn't even His idea. He hadn't planned to do it, but Mary changed His mind:

> On the third day a wedding took place at Cana in Galilee. Jesus' mother was there, and Jesus and His disciples had also been invited to the wedding. When the

wine was gone, Jesus' mother said to Him, "They have no more wine." "Woman, why do you involve Me?" Jesus replied. "My hour has not yet come." His mother said to the servants, "Do whatever He tells you." Nearby stood six stone water jars, the kind used by the Jews for ceremonial washing, each holding from twenty to thirty gallons. Jesus said to the servants, "Fill the jars with water"; so they filled them to the brim. Then He told them, "Now draw some out and take it to the master of the banquet." They did so, and the master of the banquet tasted the water that had been turned into wine (John 2:1-9).

A little piece of advice to all the guys who might be reading this book: only Jesus can go around calling His mom "woman" and get away with it. When two people in a marriage understand the type of servant leadership that Jesus modeled for us, it's easy to lead together, working as a team whose goal is to glorify God and love one another.

PROVERBS 31 WOMAN

If you are a woman and you've been a Christian for longer than three weeks, you know who "the Proverbs 31 woman" is without any need for further explanation. I've always loved reading about her, and I've always felt inspired when reading that passage of Scripture. But recently it was brought to my attention that not all women have enjoyed hearing about the Proverbs 31 woman because they feel like she is a lot to measure up to. I would like to address that. First of all, the Proverbs 31 woman isn't an actual woman. When King Lemuel was still a young prince, his mother created a type of poem to help him know what kind of a virtuous wife he should seek. This poem made it into our Scripture canon, and we now know of this portion of Scripture as the Book of Proverbs, chapter 31. Let's take a look together, and then I want to tell you why I love it. To me, Proverbs 31 is an excellent example of a healthy, egalitarian marriage.

A wife of noble character who can find? She is worth far more than rubies. Her husband has full confidence in her and lacks nothing of value. She brings him good, not harm, all the days of her life. She selects wool and flax and works with eager hands. She is like the merchant ships, bringing her food from afar. She gets up while it is still night; she provides food for her family and portions for her female servants. She considers a field and buys it; out of her earnings she plants a vineyard. She sets about her work vigorously; her arms are strong for her tasks. She sees that her trading is profitable, and her lamp does not go out at night. In her hand she holds the distaff and grasps the spindle with her fingers. She opens her arms to the poor and extends her hands to the needy. When it snows, she has no fear for her household; for all of them are clothed in scarlet. She makes coverings for her bed; she is clothed in fine linen and purple. Her husband is respected at the city gate, where he takes his seat among the elders of the land. She makes linen garments and sells them, and supplies the merchants with sashes. She is clothed with strength and dignity; she can laugh at the days to come. She speaks with wisdom, and faithful instruction is on her tongue. She watches over the affairs of her household and does not eat the bread of idleness. Her children arise and call her blessed; her husband also, and he praises her: "Many women do noble things, but you surpass them all." Charm is deceptive, and beauty is fleeting; but a woman who fears the LORD is to be praised. Honor her for all that her hands have done, and let her works bring her praise at the city gate (Proverbs 31:10-31).

We should not let ourselves be intimidated by this made-up woman. What we should do is realize that King Lemuel's mother wanted him to be wise when choosing a wife; therefore, she gave him characteristics to help him locate a virtuous wife. First off, what a great mom! Thank you, King Lemuel's mother, because now we have this awesome passage of Scripture.

The Proverbs 31 woman is a bold, confident, wise, and business-savvy woman. She considers a field and buys it? Wait...she doesn't call her husband first and ask his permission? It sounds like she is also a decision maker in her marriage.

Out of HER earnings, she plants a vineyard. Wait...she has earnings? You mean she's not a full-time homeschool mom who quietly stifles all her opinions and individuality? Nope. I dare you to read this portion of Scripture and admire how bold and strong she is while still being feminine, godly, and lovely. Her husband trusts in her. She has so much freedom to lead and to be a strong, decision-making, business-savvy woman.

WHAT I'M ALSO NOT SAYING

Again I find it necessary to do another little episode of "what I'm not saying." I don't want women to take what I'm saying and swing the pendulum so far to the other extreme that they become intolerable. What I'm not saying is that a woman should go make huge financial decisions that she knows would upset her husband. I don't think that's very wise. I do believe a couple can grow in trust to the point where this is absolutely possible, both ways. For now, I believe that each couple should agree on what works for them right now.

Obviously, not all of us are in the position to just go out and buy a field (or a Michael Kors purse) without consulting our significant other. I'm not saying that a woman should try to be an independent agent who doesn't need her husband and scoffs at his help. That type of attitude isn't beneficial to a marriage. The beauty of marriage is that we GET to live with our best friend...forever! Your relationship with your spouse may not exactly be at BFF status right now, but please do not give up hope. Keep moving forward, keep trusting God, and keep purposefully loving the man or woman that God has given you.

No matter what, at the end of the day, submission is a choice. No spouse—neither husband nor wife—should have the goal to make his or her spouse submit. Submission is a two-way street for every couple that loves and respects one another. Two-way submission is biblical, and I hope in this chapter I was able to give you something new to consider.

Chapter 8

UNDERSTANDING HEADSHIP

Ironically enough, one day, while preparing for the writing of this book, I stumbled upon a quite graphic picture on Kris Vallotton's Facebook page that mentioned something about male headship. I can't remember the quote or the picture, but I do remember this one lady's comment: "No man will ever be the head of me! That's not for me." Now, let me just surprise everyone for a second and say that I know how she feels. I really, deeply feel this woman. I just saw her tiny little thumbnail pic as I was scrolling on my iPhone, but I feel her, man. I don't really want a man being the "head" of me in the way that our culture defines "head." Hint: we are defining the word very differently than the word is actually defined. I can show you how.

Before we go any further, I want us to take a look together at the Scriptures that are causing all the uproar. All of these verses were written by the Apostle Paul.

> *For the husband is the head* (kephalē) *of the wife as Christ is the head* (kephalē) *of the church, His body, of which He is the Savior* (Ephesians 5:23).

But I want you to realize that the head (kephalē) of every man is Christ, and the head (kephalē) of the woman is man, and the head (kephalē) of Christ is God (1 Corinthians 11:3).

He is also the head of the church, which is His body. He is the beginning, the first come back to life so that He would have first place in everything (Colossians 1:18 GW).

First of all, let's consider this: If man is the head of woman, then Christ is the head of man, and God is the head of Christ, so then is Christ inferior to God? With the way our culture thinks of the word *head*, this is the obvious conclusion. The answer to that is no, this verse isn't trying to say that Christ is inferior to God, man is inferior to Christ, and that women are inferior to men. That is just not what is being said here. The meaning is being "lost in translation," so to speak, because of the strange ideas our culture has about "the head" meaning "the big boss."

I will elaborate because my goal here is to bring you some clarity on this and not more confusion.

The English language defines the word *head* as "that thing sitting on top of your neck," or "the boss, the one in charge of things." In the Greek being used here, *kephalē*—can I just let you in on a little secret?—*head* doesn't mean "boss" in this context. God didn't give people the right to have control over other people. God gave people authority to rule and reign over the powers of darkness.

In modern-day English, we often use the word *head* metaphorically to represent the leader of an organization. Is it possible, then, that in this passage of Scripture, Paul is using the word *head* (*kephalē*) metaphorically as well? Well, he sure as sugar isn't using the word literally. If he were, then he would literally be saying that

God is actually Christ's physical head. To my knowledge, nobody anywhere interprets this literally. Scholars across the board agree this is metaphorical. No matter what, it is a metaphor. It's just a matter of us figuring out which metaphor fits better based on scriptural and historical context, what agrees with the character of the writer, and what agrees with the message of the Bible. Since each of these verses is written by Paul, whichever metaphor is being used in one verse is the same one being used in the others.

I believe that Paul's objective here was to show God as the source of all life. God gave life to Jesus through Mary. God gave life to man. The first man, Adam, was created by God, and then God took one of his ribs and created Eve. She was called woman because she came "out of man."

> So the Lord God caused the man to fall into a deep sleep; and while he was sleeping, He took one of the man's ribs and then closed up the place with flesh. Then the Lord God made a woman from the rib He had taken out of the man, and He brought her to the man. The man said, "This is now bone of my bones and flesh of my flesh; she shall be called 'woman,' for she was taken out of man" (Genesis 2:21-23)"

This is another very interesting and plausible perspective with which I very much agree. Catherine Clark Kroeger, PhD, wrote very convincingly in order to give us enough insight from ancient philosophers to give me enough to believe that it would have been historically understood that the metaphor Paul was using was that of a "head" of a river. I want you to read firsthand what she had to say:

> In the case of "head," we have strong indications of the definition as it was understood by the ancients. Homer called

the innermost part of a stream its "head," while Eusthatius explained that the river's head is that which generates the whole river. Herodotus tells of a river that rose from thirty-eight separate sources or "heads." Philoponus, in the sixth century a.d., noted that a river, when it rushed upon a rock, might divide and become two streams, even though it had but a single source (kephalē), and the medical writer Galen observed that a river arising from a single spring might be larger at the "head" (kephalē) than farther down along its banks. The Digest of Justinian declared authoritatively, "The head is the place whence the water issues forth."

Not only with respect to flowing water was the head considered the place of beginning. Aristotle himself declared that the head was the source or beginning of life, with human sperm being created in the head, traveling down the spinal cord, flowing into the genitals, and so procreating the human race. Thus, the ancient writers sometimes referred to sexual intercourse as "diminishing one's head." Artemidorus of Ephesus maintained that the head was like one's father because, just as the head was the source of light and life for the whole body, so a father was the source of life for his son. "The head is like one's parents because it is the source or cause of one's having life." Shortly after the New Testament period, Plutarch told of those who thought the brain "to be the source of generation." Philo, a Jewish contemporary of Jesus and Paul, wrote, "As though he were the head of a living being, Esau is the progenitor of all those members who have been mentioned."

Among other values, the head as the source of paternity was understood by the early Christian fathers. Irenaeus equates "head" with "source" when he writes of the "head and source of his own being." Hippolytus emphasized the productivity of this bodily member when he designated the head as the characteristic substance from which all people were made. He noted, "In the head is said to be the brain, formulating the being from which all fatherhood is produced." Cosmas Indicopleustes (sixth century A.D.) called Adam the "head" of all people in this world because he was their source and father.

Photius, a ninth century Byzantine scholar, was renowned for his vast knowledge of classical authors and his preservation of numerous quotations from works that are now lost to us. He drew upon earlier scholars passionately committed to preserving classical Greek and promoting a continued knowledge of its words and forms. These works Photius edited and incorporated into a formidable lexicon intended as a reference book to aid later writers in understanding the vocabulary of classical and sacred authors. He quite specifically stated that "head" was considered to be a synonym for procreator or progenitor....

An Orphic fragment probably from the sixth century b.c., declares: Zeus was born first, Zeus last, god of the bright bolt: Zeus is the head [kephalē], Zeus the middle, from Zeus are all things made. Sometimes, however, the last line runs, "Zeus the beginning [archē], Zeus the middle, and Zeus the end." Four times Zeus is called head, kephalē, and three times archē, source or beginning. Thus, the two terms appear synonymous in this context, as has been noted by various classical scholars....

Other artistic representations sometimes depict the head as productive of growing life. The myth of Athena springing from the head of Zeus is known in story form, mosaics, frescoes, and vase paintings. Ancient Orphic burials sometimes contained figurines of the soul reemerging into the world after remaining nine years beneath the bosom of Persephone, queen of the dead. From the head of the goddess sprout up new little heads, some surrounded by leaf buds as they grow to full reincarnation status. The theme of head as starting point for growth is unmistakable.

Thus, St. Augustine declared love to be the head that produced all the other Christian virtues. From its fertile soil sprang the rest of the spiritual graces....

Exactly this concept of growth is what we find explicated by the Apostle Paul in Colossians 2:19 and Ephesians 4:15-16, his two sole passages dealing with the function of the head in relation to the body. In both of these passages, he maintains that the head not only causes growth but also causes the body to build itself up. A more expanded paraphrase might read as follows: Paul gives very nearly the same concept when he turns to the relationship of head and body in Ephesians chapter 4, certainly a passage to take very seriously when we are considering Ephesians chapter 5. The Apostle wrote: Let us grow up in all things unto Him who is Christ, the Head. He causes the body to build itself up in love as the head provides empowerment according to the proportion appropriate for each member as they are bound and supported by every sinew (Eph. 4:15-16, the author's translation).

Frequently, we assume that the Bible uses "head" to imply "boss" or "chief," and so we miss the assurance of this passage. Here the focus is on the function of the head in producing growth. Every part of the body is connected to the head, and, if the connecting nerve is severed, even a perfectly healthy member will wither. But every part is also interconnected to every other part, and each has a different function that causes it to depend on every other member....

Medical writers considered the head as the crucial element in treating the entire body. Aetius Amidenus Medicus insisted that a physician must always begin with the head, because it was the root and source of the entire bodily condition. If the head was indisposed, then the whole body was affected. Aretaeus wrote, "From the head is the source of life, because the head is the place of perception and the starting point of the nerves." Philo announced that the limbs of the body draw life from the forces in the head. The commonly held anatomical view of antiquity, that the head was the source of the body's existence, led the foremost exegete of the early church to further metaphorical uses.

From the head, John Chrysostom said, the senses "have their source and fount": In the head are the eyes both of the body, and of the soul.... All the senses have thence their origin and source. Thence are sent forth the organs of speech, the power of seeing and of smelling, and all touch. For thence is derived the root of the nerves and bones. Athanasius stated, "For the head (which is the source) of all things is the Son, but God is the head (which is the source) of Christ." Cyril, Archbishop of Alexandria, wrote of Adam: Therefore of our race he became first head, which is source, and was of the earth and earthy. Since Christ was named the second Adam, He has been placed as head, which is source, of those who through Him have been formed anew unto Him unto immortality through sanctification in the Spirit....[9]

Below is another excerpt from the writings of Kroeger, who is now deceased, but who was the founder of CBE, Christians for Biblical Equality:

Proponents of a hierarchical view of the sexes will argue that woman is of a secondary order of creation over whom man is the "head" [kephale] and that therefore she must "submit." The Bible does indeed say that the man is head of the woman, Christ head of the man, and God the head of Christ (1 Corinthians 11:3). Saint John Chrysostom, an early Greek Father and a highly influential exegete of Scripture, was aware of the theological implications of ascribing inferiority to any member of the Godhead. Therefore he declared that anyone was a heretic who proclaimed that "head" in this context denoted superior power or authority! Let us be aware that a metaphor is just that—a figure of speech used to enforce a concept. Furthermore, metaphors may change meaning in different languages and cultures.

In French, for instance, "head" does not have the meaning of "boss" or "chief" as it does in English. In ancient Greek, the original language in which the New Testament was written, "head" very seldom denoted a person in a position of power or superiority. Obviously its first meaning was that of a body part, one dependent on and interactive with the rest of the body. Its earliest use as a metaphor was as a term of endearment, to denote an individual to whom one directed strong emotion. In the Odyssey, Odysseus calls his wife

Penelope his "head." Head might mean the entire person, just as we speak in English of a "head count." Greek writers utilized a concept of the head as source of life. Aristotle and many another Greeks believed that sperm was formed in the head, while ancient physicians considered the head to be the source of every bodily condition. The Apostle Paul recognized man as the source of woman, and woman as the source of man and called for mutual support and interdependence in the Lord (see 1 Corinthians 11:8-12).

The doctrine of headship is egregiously misapplied when it comes to assignment of decision-making roles. All too often husband and wife both believe that the husband is to make the ultimate decisions in matters profoundly affecting the lives of the entire family. Yet this is not the way that God treats us nor the way Christ deals with His bride, the Church. By God's own design, each one of us has been given free will. It is up to us whether or not we shall worship God, study the Word, follow after righteousness, do acts of kindness, and lead others to Christ and so on. If there is no compulsion in Christ's dealing with us, why do we introduce such a mandatory element into husband-wife relationships? Christ calls us not as puppets but as fully responsible persons, free and capable of making our own decisions. He says that we are not servants but friends. If we deprive the wife of the right to have her opinions heard and respected, if we do not encourage her to become mature in decision-making, how can we say that the marriage reflects the relationship between Christ and the Church?[10]

I think it's really simple to prove that Paul's metaphor definitely wasn't that men are to be the boss of women and in charge of their wives. If Paul was trying to say that men are "the heads of women" in the sense that they "have the last say," or to say that men are to lead their wives only, at all times, then it would be a major contradiction to First Corinthians 7:4:

> *The wife does not have authority over her own body,*
> *but the husband does; and likewise also the husband does*
> *not have authority over his own body, but the wife does*
> (NASB).

Paul wrote Corinthians. If by "head" Paul was trying to say that husbands are "in charge" or that they have the last say, then that would be a contradiction of this other statement he said. To me, it's obvious that Paul isn't contradicting himself, but rather that many people have isolated the verses about headship and picked a meaning for "head" that contradicts Paul's other statement here in First Corinthians 7:4.

When interpreting Scripture, if our interpretation contradicts another part of the Bible, then it just seems like common sense to me that somewhere there's a misunderstanding and that we should definitely take a closer look. This is one of those cases.

Furthermore, nowhere in Scripture does it state that the man/ husband in a family is the "head of the household." I believe that this statement is taking the information about headship in Scripture and applying a modern understanding, violating the original meaning and intent.

Both a man and a woman come to a marriage with a lot to offer. The man has strengths and weaknesses. The woman has strengths and weaknesses. This couple would be wise to utilize each of their strengths to forge a powerful alliance. They can successfully lead together. In many ways, they are both leaders in their own regard.

This completely fits well with Ephesians 5:21, which says, *"Submit to one another out of reverence to Christ."* For example, maybe the wife has a knack for administrative tasks. She can put a budget together in a way that her husband says, "boggles his mind." Would this couple not be wise to decide that the wife leads this area? Well, if they were both taught a misapplication of Scripture their whole lives, they might be inclined to struggle along with the husband "in charge" of the finances, even though it is not his strength. A wise couple will capitalize on each other's strengths, letting one spouse support the other where that spouse is weak and allowing him or her to take the lead in other areas. There's nothing wrong with that.

My husband and I are friends with a dear couple. For years, the wife worked outside the home with a professional job that brought in a very good income, while the husband stayed at home with their two children. This couple loves God very much, and they see that as a team, they would be wise not to follow cultural gender stereotypes but rather to be led by the Holy Spirit and do what is right and what is smart for their family in that season. They were both very happy and content during this season of their life. It worked very well for their family.

So many Christians have it stuck in their head that a man is supposed to be "the head of the **household**" when that's not even in Scripture. The Bible does talk about a man being the head of his wife, but I hope that I brought some real clarity to this in this chapter.

Each culture has its way of talking and saying things, and it's very important, if we're to understand properly what God is trying to say to us through Scripture, that we examine these sayings from the perspective of the people who wrote them and from the perspective of whom they were originally written for.

I hope the lady in the comment thread of the Kris Valloton post that I mentioned at the beginning of this chapter, manages somehow to get her hands on this book.

Chapter 9

THE COST OF TRAILBLAZING

believe the message I've included in this book is very important and that it is imperative for the Church to hear it in this hour. In advancing the Kingdom, it is vital that the Church at large make room for women. I spent seven years being a Christian before anyone would really invest in me as a believer by truly discipling me and equipping me for the works of ministry. For many years I believed I had a calling on my life, but I didn't know how I'd ever become trained to fulfill that calling. I trusted that God would make a way, though, and He did.

The goal of this book is to set people free and equip people. I hope it did that for you. Also, this book is me calling you out. I'm calling you out to be a part of God's Feminist Movement. You don't have to call yourself a feminist. I know that for many people, that's just not a term with which they wish to associate themselves, and that's really okay. I ask you to be brave with me and be a part of God's Feminist Movement. Let's blaze a trail for the women who will follow behind us.

It won't always be easy. Many years ago, before I was even born again, my aunt, who is a mighty woman of God, prophesied over me that I would one day be a trailblazer and that I would do great things for God. She had no basis for that word of prophecy, based on what she could see with her physical eyes. In the natural, I was on a slippery slope of sin and destructive behavior. Tangled up in addiction, drugs, and promiscuity, there was no indicator (in the natural) that I would ever be able to get free and fulfill that prophecy.

Fast-forward many years later, and some pretty remarkable things have happened. Not only did I become born again at twenty-one, but at twenty-three my husband and I stepped into the unknown as youth pastors. I look back on those years, and now I see that we, unbeknownst to us, had stepped into God's "accelerated program." And by "accelerated" I mean that God did more inner healing in me in one year than I thought humanly possible. I made the transition from ministering out of guilt and obligation to being compelled by love and compassion. I grew and blossomed in ways I never even knew possible. I began to receive revelations of love from the Father, and chains of bondage melted like wax. I never even knew one could be as free as I was, yet there I was, being led by the Holy Spirit out of the captivity that only months ago I had not known I even needed to be freed from.

Many experiences shaped who I am today, but I will never forget each time God called me out of my comfort zone. Eventually, our journey with the Lord brought us to Vinita, Oklahoma, where we were the youth pastors in a very small town. I still remember the day that Rene came to me and told me that he believed that God was calling us to leave Oklahoma and move up to Virginia to plant a church.

I was shocked at his words, and I was so angry at him for even suggesting that we leave the church at which we were working. I was comfortable! I was happy! Things were going good so why should we do anything differently? Why rock the boat?! That had to be crazy talk. Surely my husband would come to his senses soon! He said to me, "Well, just pray about it and see what God tells you." I was too mad to even pray about it, but I kept feeling the Holy Spirit bring it up, and each time He did, I felt that we were indeed to uproot and move to Virginia to plant a church. It was the strangest thing since only weeks prior, I had been perfectly content and happy living right there, doing life as usual. At this point, I prayed (possibly) one of the dumbest things I've ever prayed.

If God asks you to do something and you feel like you need a sign, I would encourage you not to pray this: "Okay God, if You want us to move to Virginia to plant a church, then You'll have to somehow make it to where I don't want to be here anymore doing this." At the time, I didn't really see what could go wrong, but after praying that, everything went wrong. I had unrest in my spirit, there was conflict everywhere we turned, and eventually it became crystal clear to me that God was answering my prayer. I came home one day bawling to my husband that I was ready to move. I couldn't handle any more confirmations!

We moved halfway across the country, and it was not an easy move. I could probably write a very long book on the problems that arose during that move, the ways that it stretched our faith and our patience, and the ways that it ultimately strengthened our bond as a family and our love for one another. I'm not sure I would even want to write such a book, though. If I had to put it into a brief statement, I would simply say that it was a time of suffering that wasn't in any way enjoyable, but now that it's over, I wouldn't trade it for anything. God used that very unenjoyable situation, and He turned it around to bless us and train us.

So here we are. In Virginia. Planting a church—Streams of Life Church.

It's pretty rockin' awesome most of the time, but I haven't always felt confident. The life of obedience isn't always easy, and there's always someone who is happy to point at you and let you know you're doing it all wrong. There are plenty of dream crushers out there, and plenty of people who will advise you to "just get a real job and quit chasing dreams." Those people are usually rational and logical people who are just trying to bring you back down to reality because they don't want to see you disappointed. I have yet to meet anyone who shared with me their life calling and I thought, "Wow. That's very rational and logical. Must be God."

When God calls you to do something, it's not to be done in the natural but in the supernatural. It's pretty rad how that works.

One night when I was particularly discouraged, I went to the Lord, and I cried out to Him. I wept before my Father and crawled into His lap. "People are so mean," I told my Daddy as tears poured down. "These sheep, they're crazy," I said to Him. I cried in His lap while He held me and allowed me to just get it all out, and after some time, God showed me a vision:

I was on a road, and Jesus was there. And He said to me, "You are at an intersection. You can choose which road you want, and I will bless either one." I looked and saw that even though Jesus was saying I was at an intersection, I only saw one road ahead of me.

Jesus then said to me, "You see that road. It's a good road, and it would make a fine choice. Many people put their blood, sweat, and tears into the paving of that road. They paid a high price. They made sacrifices, and they paved a good road."

Once again, I pointed out to Jesus that there only seemed to be one road from which I could choose. As a response, He gestured out into the wilderness, and He said, "Well, the other road, you see, hasn't been paved yet."

I cried a sea of tears that night. Before, I had been crying out of my own heartache. I had been crying because of the pain of being betrayed by people whom I loved and because of feelings of persecution. But now, the tears flowed from a deeper place, a place within me that remembered the prophetic word that my aunt had spoken over me all those years ago, even before I was born again. Suddenly, her words echoed in my spirit: "Baby, one day you're gonna do great things for the Lord. You're gonna be a trailblazer." Suddenly, it all clicked. It made sense to me that my destiny was somehow rooted in this road that wasn't even paved yet. Just then, I knew that there would always be a part of me that would never quite be fulfilled unless I took the road that hadn't even been paved yet.

I often have had to remind myself of that night with my Jesus, when He held me so tightly in His arms and reassured me of the calling on my life. Last night He reassured me that He never gets tired of reassuring me and that if I'll run into His arms each time I feel uncertain or discouraged, He will faithfully realign my perspective with His.

This has not been easy. This choice I've made to follow the Father's call has come at a cost. I knew at the beginning that it would cost everything.

I am thankful for a husband who doesn't lose sight of the calling with which the Father has entrusted us. I am undone and utterly in awe of the goodness of the Father, because though we walk through difficult places, do difficult things, and go places that others won't go, we, as a family, have terrific peace and joy that overflows and bubbles over.

You, too, have a calling on your life. It will not be easy. It won't fit the mold. It might tick people off. There will probably even be those who will try to tell you you're doing it all wrong. Listen to the Father. Make it a point to crawl into His lap and press your ear to His chest. That way, you'll always be able to dance to the rhythm of heaven. Dance on, my beautiful friend, and enjoy the melody of His grace.

I'm asking you to join with me as a trailblazer. I believe we are changing the world. I believe that when we all release God's glory in our own unique way by loving the people around us and being the change that we are called to be, then we make more than just a ripple effect. The ripple effect occurs when a tiny, little pebble that's dropped in a pond causes the water to ripple out all the way to the edge of the pond. But what will happen when you and I, and all of us, release His glory all over the earth—that's much bigger than a ripple. That, my friend, is a tidal wave. Let's get things wet.

ENDNOTES

1. "Feminism," Merriam-Webster, accessed September 14, 2015, http://www.merriam-webster.com/dictionary/feminism.

2. "Feminism," Wikipedia, last modified September 14, 2015, accessed September 14, 2015, https://en.wikipedia.org/wiki/Feminism.

3. Flavius Josephus, *The Antiquities of the Jews*, trans. William Whiston, n.d., ca. 1737, accessed September 14, 2015, http://www.documentacatholicaomnia.eu/03d/0037-0103,_Flavius_Josephus,_The_Antiquities_Of_The_Jews,_EN.pdf, 3.7.

4. Maimonides, *The Guide for the Perplexed* (Philadelphia, PA: Empire Books, 2011), 204, quoted in Jonathan Welton, *Raptureless: An Optimistic Guide to the End of the World* (Jonathan Weitem, 2013).

5. Harmon L. Smith, "William Capers and William A. Smith: Neglected Advocates of the Pro-Slavery Moral Argument," *Methodist History* (October 1964): 22-32, accessed September 16, 2015, http://archives.gcah.org/xmlui/handle/10516/1367.

6. Kyle Painter, "The Pro-Slavery Argument in the Development of the American Methodist Church," *Constructing the Past* 2.1 (2001): 29-46, accessed September 16, 2015, http://digitalcommons.iwu.edu/cgi/viewcontent.cgi?article=1061&context=constructing.

7. *Strong's Concordance*, s.v. "metanoeó," accessed September 14, 2015, http://biblehub.com/greek/3340.htm.

8. *Strong's Exhaustive Concordance*, s.v. "sózó," accessed September 14, 2015, http://biblehub.com/greek/4982.htm.

9. Catherine Clark Kroeger, "Toward an Understanding of Ancient Conceptions of 'Head,'" *Priscilla Papers* 20, no. 3 (2006): 5-6, http://www.cbeinternational.org/sites/default/files/pp203_2tauoacoh.pdf.

10. Catherine Clark Kroeger and James R. Beck, eds., *Women, Abuse, and the Bible: How Scripture Can Be Used to Hurt or to Heal* (Grand Rapids, MI: Baker Books, 1996).

ABOUT THE AUTHOR

Amber Picota serves as Pastor of Streams of Life Church alongside her husband, Rene, and homeschools their three children.

Amber loves people, writing, reading, traveling, and speaking; her greatest desire is to see people come alive as they realize who they are and discover what kind of authority and freedom they have in Christ. Amber's cutting-edge blog, amberpicota.com, features her thoughts about spirituality, motherhood, relationships, and walking in the the fullness of your New Covenant inheritance!

FREE E-BOOKS?
YES, PLEASE!

Get **FREE** and deeply-discounted **Christian books** for your **e-reader** delivered to your inbox **every week!**

IT'S SIMPLE!

VISIT lovetoreadclub.com

SUBSCRIBE by entering your email address

RECEIVE free and discounted e-book offers and inspiring articles delivered to your inbox every week!

Unsubscribe at any time.

SUBSCRIBE NOW!

LOVE TO READ CLUB

visit **LOVETOREADCLUB.COM** ▶